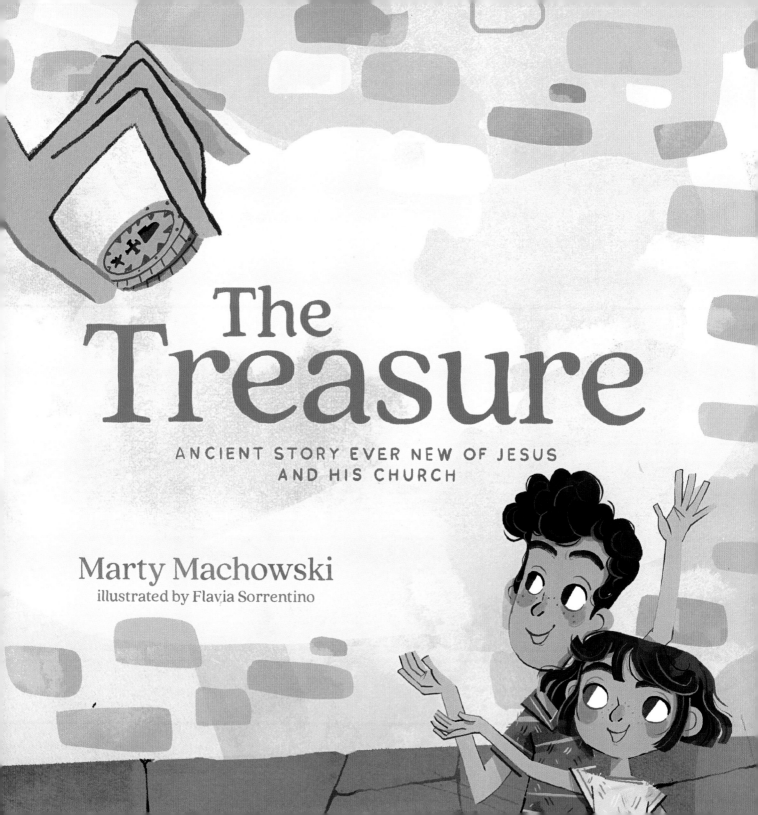

The Treasure

ANCIENT STORY EVER NEW OF JESUS
AND HIS CHURCH

Marty Machowski

illustrated by Flavia Sorrentino

New Growth Press, Greensboro, NC 27401

Text Copyright © 2023 by Marty Machowski

Illustration Copyright © 2023 by Flavia Sorrentino

Cover/Illustrations: Flavia Sorrentino

Interior Design/Typesetting: Dan Stelzer and Alecia Sharp

ISBN 978-1-64507-316-1

Library of Congress Cataloging-in-Publication Data on file LCCN 2023012904

Printed in India

31 30 29 28 27 26 25 24   2 3 4 5 6

DEDICATION

To all the parents, grandparents,
and caregivers who will read
these pages and share the treasure
of Christ with the next generation.

CONTENTS

BOOK ONE
An Adventure through Luke

BOOK TWO

An Adventure through Acts

The Treasure is designed to help children grow in knowing and loving God through reading the gospel of Luke and the book of Acts. It is my hope that in this journey of learning to apply Scripture, you will be amazed at how these two books connect.

People often think of Luke and Acts as two separate books telling two separate stories. But they are actually two halves of one greater story. Together, they work to share the singular plan of God's salvation. Luke is the only gospel writer to record the advance of the gospel beyond the ascension of our Lord into heaven. Through his retelling of the gospel story and the growth of the church, we see the Father's love in sending his Son, Jesus. We see the obedience of Christ all the way to his death upon a cross, as well as the Spirit's work in forming God's family.

To help children learn how to understand the truths of Luke and Acts, *The Treasure* follows the story of a family who is also reading through Luke's narrative. As you journey with Theos,

Mira, and Lydia, encourage your children to make personal connections in their own lives.

The Treasure is designed to be read alongside the Bible. Read the designated Scripture passage and then read the corresponding text.

This book can be appreciated by a range of ages. The text is written for elementary school ages, but the illustrations will help the youngest follow along. Also included at the end of the book is a Bible study for older children, "Connecting Luke and Acts with the Old Testament."

Finally, I want to encourage you to read this book slowly. This will help you to seek and find the hidden treasure. After all, what would an adventure be without a treasure?

Now it's time to set sail! Listen carefully. Do you hear the captain shouting, "Weigh anchor! Raise the main!"

Hold on tight: our journey has begun!

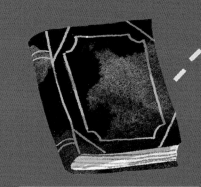

BOOK ONE

An Adventure
through the
Gospel of Luke

The Discovery

Once upon a time, on the Greek Island of Naxos, two children finished their morning chores and ran down to the sea.

Theos took a deep breath of salty sea air, as he and his sister, Mira, sought stones to throw.

Mira picked up two that lay side by side. "Here you go," she said, offering one to her brother.

Theos held the stone, turning it in his hand to find the best grip. He felt the warmth of the sun on the back of his neck as it rose above Mt. Zeus behind him.

"Let's see who can hit the water!" Mira shouted as she launched her stone. She watched it soar as the sea waves crashed against the rocky coast. Her rock fell short, clacking down into the boulders below. Theos welcomed the challenge. He ran forward to the edge of the grass and launched his stone with all his might.

The rock sailed toward the sea and almost made it to the water. But as chance would

1

have it, a sudden gust of wind returned it to shore. The stone fell short of the waves and dropped into the boulders below. It landed with a loud pop, crack, and tinkle of broken pieces. The seagulls soaring along the coast, squawked.

"Did you hear that?" asked Theos.
"I think it hit something!"

"Let's go see," replied Mira as she scrambled down the boulders. Theos followed. The smell of shellfish and seaweed wafted up from the damp rocks.

Theos scanned the area and spotted a clay jar, the size of a small barrel, wedged between two boulders, the bottom half covered by sand. "There!" Theos shouted, "Straight ahead. My stone struck a jar!" He pointed to a black hole the size of an orange, atop the vessel.

"Look," Mira said. "There's something written on it." She could see letters covered in sand.

Mira dug away at the sand. "*Pronoia Thalassa*," she read aloud. "I think it's a name. It looks like an old water jar."

"*Providence of the Sea*," Theos said, translating the name in English. Then he reached down to put his hand into the jar.

"Theo!" Mira shouted. "What if there's a snake in there?"

"Relax, Mira. The jar is sealed," he said. "Look, it's dry inside." Then Theos knelt down and reached in, all the way up to his shoulder. "There is something in here," he said. "Several pieces of paper, but I can't grab hold of them."

Theos pulled out his hand and then lifted a heavier rock with both hands above his head.

"Don't break it," Mira said.

"Too late for that," Theos replied as he released the rock, which landed with a loud crash. Theos rolled the rock aside and cleared the larger broken pieces of clay. Then he retrieved two scrolls and passed one to Mira.

Mira unrolled the scroll.

Theos leaned over and read the script aloud, "The Gospel of Luke." Then he opened the second scroll and read, "The Acts of the Apostles."

"They are Bible scrolls," Mira said. "They look old." She lifted the scroll to her nose and drew in a whiff. "They smell old," she added.

Theos reached back into the bottom of the jar and felt around. He grasped another object and retrieved a leather-bound book. His eyes opened wide, and he sat speechless as he read one word: *Treasure.*

Theos turned the cover for Mira to read.

"*The Treasure: Ancient Story Ever New of Jesus and His Church*, 1910," she read.

Theos opened the leather-bound journal and read the first page aloud:

Where it all began . . .

It is no small providence that I took aboard my father's trading ship, a man named Cristobal. I gave his missionary family free passage to Naxos. Soon after we set sail from the African coast, Cristobal introduced me to the gospel—a story from long ago, preserved upon two scrolls. Cristobal asked if he might read the scrolls to the crew each night after dinner. I did not like the idea, but when he told me the scrolls were written to a man who shared my name, Theophilus, I agreed.

The story of Jesus touched my heart and the lives of my crew. Upon our safe arrival in Naxos, he insisted I keep the scrolls as a gift. The following year, I studied these letters and realized my need for repentance.

Years before, I had taken my father's ship despite his objections. I had not been home in years. Now, convicted of my sin, I returned my father's ship to him. Like the prodigal son in the scroll, I confessed my sin to my father, and asked him to forgive me. Then I rejoined his business on the wharf. I continued serving him until a raging fire destroyed our business and took my father's life. I had nowhere to go, but Cristobal welcomed me into his home where I resumed my study of the scrolls. Now my days are short. Soon I will join my father, along with the great saints of old, worshiping the King before the throne.

To you who have discovered my bequest, I leave you the scrolls along with my journals. They record my study and include my personal illustrations.

Read each page carefully. I've placed questions for you along the way. Their answers will help you solve a riddle. Complete the riddle and you will find the location of my hidden treasure. Yes, there is a real treasure, which is yours for the taking.

Blessings on your quest,
Captain Theophilus Adamos
Providence of the Sea

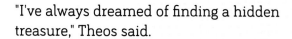

"I've always dreamed of finding a hidden treasure," Theos said.

"Do you think it's real?" Mira asked.

"Of course!" Theos answered. "It says so right here!" He held the journal in the bright shining sun.

"So, what do we do now?"

"Follow the Captain's orders!" Theos replied. If we are to discover the treasure, we've got to read the scrolls and study his journal. Then we fill in the blanks to discover the clue. And that, will . . ."

"Lead us to the treasure!" shouted Mira and Theos together.

Further up the hill, a man and his dog stood watching. He turned to his dog and said, "That jar sat hidden for a long time, Salty." He stroked Salty's fur. "They found it on their own, without the help of the lost coin." Salty turned toward his master and let out a sharp bark.

"Yes, I do think we need to pay them a visit," the man said to Salty. "But let's give them a week or two to get into the story."

Salty barked again.

As Pastor Thomas walked along the path that led up the hill to a church, he said, "I never would have guessed they would find the jar on their own. Must be providence. The Captain would be pleased."

As the only pastor living in the area, Thomas watched over Theos and Mira's family. Since their father had passed away and they didn't attend church, Pastor Thomas often visited them and shared extra garden produce with them.

"The Lord loves that family," Pastor Thomas said as he walked toward home. Then he turned back to catch one last glimpse of the kids.

He watched as the two children topped the last rolling hill and disappeared from sight.

When Theos and Mira returned home, they climbed into the hayloft of the barn and carefully opened the scrolls. They read through them for most of the morning, trying to answer each question they encountered.

And now, dear reader,
it's your turn.

The very same book Theos and Mira discovered
in that old water jar, is now in your hands.
It comes not by chance, but by the hand of
providence. Read it alongside the gospel of
Luke and the book of Acts. Study its pages, and
you too will find the clues to solve the riddle.
The riddle will lead you to the treasure—
the treasure of Theophilus.

· PART ONE ·

The Story Begins

The gospel of Luke was most likely written 30 to 40 years after Jesus lived on earth. Luke was not an original disciple of Jesus and likely never met him. Luke, a doctor, traveled with the apostle Paul—every so often the words "we" and "us" will appear in Acts, showing the author, Luke, was present [see Acts 16:10, for example]). Paul called Luke his "fellow worker" (Philemon 1:24) and "beloved physician"; also, he described Luke as well-loved (Colossians 4:14). The gospel of Luke and its sequel, the Acts of the Apostles, make up nearly one-third of the New Testament—more than all the writings of the apostle Paul combined.

Luke opens his gospel with a short note to a man named Theophilus, sharing how and why he wrote his gospel. He wants to share the story of Jesus. Luke begins with a detailed account of the events around the time of Jesus's birth and childhood. Without Luke's gospel, we wouldn't know of the angels' announcement to the shepherds, or that Jesus was born in a stable and laid in a manger. Luke is the only gospel writer to include these parts of the story.

We will begin our study of Luke by taking a closer look at these early stories. Study Luke's gospel carefully and you will discover the key to eternal life.

Theophilus

Did you ever receive a card or letter in the mail? Before email and texting, people wrote letters to one another with paper and ink. Did you know that some of the books of the Bible are letters? The apostle Paul wrote to fellow workers, like Titus and Timothy, and to the churches he visited, like the one in Philippi. The letters were saved and carefully copied to share with others. Today, many of these letters are preserved in the Bible for us to read. The gospel of Luke is one of those letters, written to Luke's friend Theophilus.

Theophilus, whose Greek name means friend of God, lived when Christians were being arrested, beaten, and even killed. Luke wrote his friend to encourage him that Jesus's story was true and trustworthy.

Because Matthew and John were among the original twelve disciples of Jesus, their gospels likely transpired naturally—like the telling of a familiar story. They simply wrote down what they remembered. But Luke was not among the original disciples. Thus, he had to do careful research and talk to the people who knew and followed Jesus—those who heard his teaching and watched him heal the sick and perform other miracles.

As you begin this study, replace the name *Theophilus* with your own name. For God made sure that Luke's letters were passed down through the ages for you to read, too!

The Birth of John

The longer you must wait for something special, the more excited you are when it finally arrives. We get excited for birthdays, holidays, and the start of summer vacation. Now just imagine how excited the people of Israel were to finally meet God's prophet!

The last book of the Old Testament, Malachi, ends with a prophecy that God would send the prophet Elijah. The prophecy says that God would use Elijah to "turn the hearts of fathers to their children and the hearts of children to their fathers" (Malachi 4:6). But four hundred years passed before God fulfilled that promise. That's a long time!

Luke tells us that God sent an angel to a man named Zechariah. The angel announced that Zechariah's wife, Elizabeth, would have a son, and they should name him John. God said that John would come in the "spirit and power of Elijah, to turn the hearts of the fathers to the children" (Luke 1:17). After John's birth, Zechariah, through the Holy Spirit, prophesied that God would raise up a "horn of salvation" (Jesus) (v. 69), and Zechariah's son would grow up to be a prophet who would announce the coming of Jesus the Messiah (vv. 76–77). With that, the stage was set for God to fulfill another promise: the arrival of the promised Savior.

CAPTAIN'S NOTE Some people thought Jesus was Elijah (Luke 9:19). But Jesus revealed that John the Baptist was the "Elijah" God had promised to send (Matthew 11:14).

A Son and a Savior

Have you ever been startled when someone sneaks up on you? Your whole body jolts with surprise! Imagine getting a sudden visit from an angel who appears out of nowhere! No wonder Mary was frightened when Gabriel appeared in her living room!

After calming her fears, Gabriel gave Mary the most amazing news. Even though she was not yet married, she would give birth to a son by the power of the Holy Spirit. The baby was to be given the name *Jesus*. Gabriel said Jesus would sit on the throne of his far-off grandfather David and rule as king forever. He would be called the Holy Son of God. As proof that nothing was impossible for God, Gabriel told Mary that her cousin Elizabeth, who had never been able to have a baby, was now six months pregnant. Mary agreed to God's plan, for she believed the angel. Then she went to visit Elizabeth.

As Mary walked through the door and greeted her cousin, she could see Elizabeth was pregnant, just as the angel had said. The baby inside Elizabeth leapt. The Holy Spirit filled Elizabeth and revealed that Mary was pregnant too! Elizabeth greeted Mary with a blessing.

Mary in turn praised God saying, "My soul magnifies the Lord, and my spirit rejoices in God my Savior" (Luke 1:46–47). Mary knew that God chose her to give birth to the Messiah who would be her Savior and fulfill God's promise to Abraham that through him all families on earth would be blessed (see Genesis 12:3). Mary's son Jesus later fulfilled that promise by dying on the cross and rising in victory over sin and death. People from every nation who turn from their sin and believe in Jesus, are blessed with forgiveness and welcomed into God's family.

The Christmas Story

People all around the world have different Christmas traditions. Children in Iceland set their boots on a windowsill to be filled with candy. In France, kids set their shoes near the fireplace. In the United States, people decorate trees with lights and hang up stockings. But all of this gift-giving at Christmas began with the very first Christmas gift—when God gave us his only Son Jesus to be born in Bethlehem.

Did you know that Luke is the only gospel writer to tell the Christmas story? Matthew records the visit of the wise men, but says they came later, after Jesus was already born (Matthew 2:1). The gospel of Luke is the only gospel to mention the census, no room in the inn, and the story of Mary giving birth in a stable. Luke is also the only gospel writer to report the angels visiting the shepherds and proclaiming,

"Unto you is born this day in the city of David a Savior, who is Christ the Lord" (Luke 2:11). Luke wanted everyone to know that Jesus is the Messiah God promised to send.

The angels gave Jesus three titles: Savior, Christ, and Lord. The name *Savior* means deliverer. It tells us that the baby has come to rescue and save. The name *Christ* means Messiah or God's chosen one—the one the prophets promised. The prophet Micah foretold of a great King who would shepherd God's people, Israel, and be born in Bethlehem (Micah 5:2–4). Jesus is the one Micah promised God would send. The name *Lord* means master, and tells us that Jesus has authority; he rules over all. When the shepherds told Mary the message given by the angels, she treasured it in her heart (Luke 2:19).

READ Luke 2:21–38

The Holy Spirit Working

Here is a riddle for you: You can't see me, but you can watch what I do. You can't touch me, but you feel when I come. Who am I? (The wind.) You can't see the wind, but you can watch it blow the leaves. You can't touch the wind, but you can feel its breeze. The Bible tells us the Holy Spirit is like the wind (John 3:8). You can't see the Holy Spirit, but you can experience his power.

More than any other gospel writer, Luke records the most about the Holy Spirit's work through Jesus. So far, Luke has reported that the Holy Spirit was with John the Baptist as a baby (Luke 1:15). He came upon Mary to conceive the baby Jesus (v. 35), filled Elizabeth at Mary's visit (v. 41), and filled Zechariah at the birth of his son (v. 67).

In today's story, Luke tells us that the Holy Spirit was at work again as Mary and Joseph brought the baby Jesus to the temple. The Holy Spirit came upon Simeon (2:25) and promised him that he would see the "Lord's Christ" (v. 26). The name Christ means God's Anointed One, the promised Messiah. Then, on just the right day and at the right time, the Spirit of God led Simeon to the temple (v. 27) to speak a prophetic blessing over the baby Jesus.

When Simeon saw Jesus, he knew he was the Promised One. He took the baby in his arms and prayed a blessing. Simeon said that Jesus would bring salvation to Israel, and be a light to the Gentiles. Simeon gave a hint to the death of Jesus when he told Mary that a sword would also pierce her soul. How did he know these things? The Spirit of God revealed them to him.

CAPTAIN'S NOTE Read Genesis 1:2 and you will see the Holy Spirit participating in the creation of the world.

My Father's House

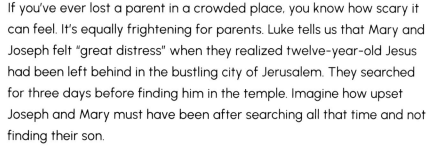

If you've ever lost a parent in a crowded place, you know how scary it can feel. It's equally frightening for parents. Luke tells us that Mary and Joseph felt "great distress" when they realized twelve-year-old Jesus had been left behind in the bustling city of Jerusalem. They searched for three days before finding him in the temple. Imagine how upset Joseph and Mary must have been after searching all that time and not finding their son.

But did you notice that Jesus wasn't worried? His reply to Mary and Joseph in Luke 2:49 gives us a clue as to why he was so calm. Jesus said, "Did you not know that I must be in my Father's house?" Mary and Joseph were upset because they could not find their son; they thought he was lost. But Jesus wasn't lost. He was in his Father's house. Even as a boy, Jesus knew that God was his Father.

Jesus also told his parents that he "must" be in his Father's house. This is a word we will see again and again in Luke's gospel. The word *must* tells us that the events in Jesus's life were not random. Jesus *must* be in his Father's house, he *must* preach the good news (Luke 4:43), and he *must* suffer, die, and be raised on the third day (9:22). Why? Because it is all a part of God's plan (Acts 2:23).

Live Like Jesus

After sharing the story of Jesus getting left behind at the temple, Luke gives us one final sentence about Jesus's childhood. He tells us that Jesus grew in wisdom, stature and favor with God and man.

Stature is a word that describes the way people see us, both inside and out. When we walk in wisdom, our stature grows, and when we act foolishly, it decreases. When you see the word stature, think of a statue of a tall warrior, wise and strong. When you study God's Word and make wise choices, you grow in stature.

As you do these things, you also grow in favor among God and man. David described God's favor like the protection of a shield in battle (Psalm 5:12). Growing in favor among people means that they welcome you, enjoy you, and are willing to help when you're in trouble.

So, live like Jesus. He studied God's Word and made wise choices based on what he learned. If you do the same, you will bless others and God will be your protection through every battle.

CAPTAIN'S NOTE

The best way to grow in wisdom is to read and study God's Word. That is what Jesus did when he remained back at the temple (Luke 2:46). The writer of Psalm 119 tells us, "Your commands make me wiser than my enemies, for they are my constant guide" (v. 98 NLT).

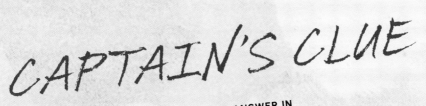

CAPTAIN'S CLUE

SEARCH FOR THE ANSWER IN

LUKE PART ONE: THE STORY BEGINS

CLUE:

To find the missing word,
reread what you read.
But this time remember,
the word that I said.

If you study Luke's gospel carefully

you will _ _ s _ _ _ _ _ r the key to eternal life.

_ _ s _ _ _ _ _ r is the first word of the riddle

you need to find my treasure.

Look What We Found!

Theos and Mira sat in the hayloft. They took turns reading aloud from the scroll of Luke.

"This is so cool," Mira said when Theos read the part where the angel Gabriel appeared to Mary. "It's the Christmas story!" she shouted.

As Theos continued reading, Mira followed along in the Captain's journal, but didn't stop to write down answers to their questions. That could wait. For now, they kept reading.

"Theos, Mira, time for lunch!" Lydia called from the kitchen. *Where are those two?* she wondered. When no one answered, she cupped her hands over her mouth and called toward the quarry, "Timotheos! Mira!" The bright white marble cliffs returned her call, echoing for miles.

Theos quickly replied, "Coming, Mom!" A moment later, he and Mira raced to the kitchen. Mira exclaimed, "You'll never believe what we found!"

Lydia smiled and thought to herself, *They play all day and never run out of energy. What have they gotten themselves into now?* Mira revealed the scrolls. "Wash your hands first," said Lydia. "Lunch is ready."

Theos held up the journal for his mother to see. Lydia took it and opened it to the Captain's introduction. "*Providence of the Sea*," she read aloud. "Never heard of it."

After washing their hands, Theos and Mira devoured Lydia's delicious gyros.

"Where did you two get this book?" Lydia asked.

Coming up for air between bites, Theos answered, "We found it in a ship's water jar, wedged in the rocks, covered with sand. Down by the sea. Do you want to read it with us?"

"An old ship's water jar?" Lydia looked at the handwritten journal, amazed at their find.

Mira added, "There's a treasure, too! You've got to study the scrolls to find it."

Lydia carefully flipped through the pages. She'd been searching for an activity to keep the kids busy during the summer. Reading the Captain's journal was the perfect solution!

Lydia continued, "Sure, we can read through it together. But you still have your summer chores. Four rows every morning," she said. Lydia drove an old tractor to till the rows of potatoes on their farm, but the weeds needed to be hoed by hand. A little work made all the difference.

"Can we start reading today?" Mira asked. "We already did our chores."

"All right," Lydia agreed. "Let's clear the table first." She, too, was eager to begin.

After removing the dishes from the table, Lydia opened the journal and began reading aloud. The children didn't mind restarting. They listened carefully as their mom read, and this time, they wrote down the answers to the Captain's questions. They searched for any clue that could lead them to the treasure.

· PART TWO ·

Prepare the Way

After Luke's account of Jesus's birth and a story from his childhood, Luke skips past Jesus's teen years. He picks up the story when Jesus is a young man and about to begin his ministry. Luke says that Jesus was "about thirty years of age" (Luke 3:23). We don't have any record of Jesus's teenage years in any of the other Gospels, or of his life through his twenties. Perhaps one day in heaven, Mary and Joseph can fill in the gaps and tell us what it was like watching Jesus grow up.

Luke jumps ahead in the life of John the Baptist, too. We go from John as a baby, to him as a grown man serving as a prophet in the wilderness. John challenged the people to repent, which means to turn away from sin. John told them it was not good to say you believe, but then live a life of sin. John called the religious rulers who came to listen to him, snakes. He ordered them to turn from their sin. John even challenged Herod, the ruler of Galilee. That got him thrown in prison (Luke 3:20), but not before he completed his mission to prepare a way for Jesus.

John the Baptist

A herald travels ahead of a king to make an announcement—to prepare people for who was coming. "Make way for the king!" they would shout, sometimes with trumpets. John the Baptist was the herald God sent to announce the start of Jesus's ministry.

The prophet Isaiah told of a day when a voice in the wilderness would announce the coming of God's Messiah. Isaiah said he would "prepare the way of the Lord" (Isaiah 40:3a). By quoting Isaiah's prophecy, Luke wants us to know John is the messenger God sent (Luke 3:2) to announce the coming of the King—King Jesus! John told everyone to get ready by turning away from their sin and turning back to love and serve the Lord.

Some thought John was the Anointed One or Messiah. But John corrected them saying, "I am not the Christ, but I have been sent before him" (John 3:28b). "I baptize you with water, but he who is mightier than I is coming, the strap of whose sandals I am not worthy to untie. He will baptize you with the Holy Spirit and fire" (Luke 3:16).

When the day came for Jesus to start his ministry, John saw him and shouted, "Behold, the Lamb of God, who takes away the sin of the world!" (John 1:29b). John wanted everyone to know that Jesus was God's chosen Lamb—the one who would die in our place so that our sins could be forgiven.

 **CAPTAIN'S NOTE**

It is helpful to compare what each gospel writer tells us about an event. Read Matthew 3, John 1:19-34, and John 3:22-30 to learn more about John the Baptist.

The Baptism of Jesus

Parents often cheer on their kids when they play sports, perform in a concert, or take part in a competition. When a child steps up to the plate in their very first baseball game, they will often hear their parent cheer from the stands. That is exactly what God the Father did when Jesus rose from the water at his baptism. He wanted everyone to know that Jesus was his Son, and that his ministry was about to begin.

All four gospel writers include the baptism of Jesus in their gospels. John tells us that the heavens opened and the Holy Spirit came down and rested upon Jesus in the form of a dove (John 1:32). The Holy Spirit was there to cheer Jesus on, too! Luke describes it like this: "the heavens were opened, and the Holy Spirit descended on [Jesus] in bodily form, like a dove; and a voice came from heaven, 'You are my beloved Son; with you I am well pleased'" (Luke 3:21–22).

When people repent of their sin and believe, they are baptized to show they are turning from their sin to follow God. So why was Jesus baptized? He didn't have any sins. Even John didn't want to baptize Jesus at first (Matthew 3:14). But Jesus told him that it was important. You see, Jesus took our sin upon himself and died in our place so that we could go to heaven. His baptism marks the beginning of his ministry rescuing sinners like us. That's why God the Father and the Holy Spirit were absolutely delighted.

The Family Tree

A family tree is one way to picture family history. A person starts out as a trunk with two branches—one for each parent. From there, each parent branch divides into smaller branches that represent grandparents, then great-grandparents, and even great, great-grandparents. People make family trees so their family history is not forgotten. Who is included in your family tree?

Luke records Jesus's family tree to show that Jesus was a far-off grandson of King David. This makes him worthy to take the throne. Luke continues the genealogy back to Abraham, to show that God's promise to bless the nations could be fulfilled through Jesus. Then Luke records the family history of Jesus all the way back to Adam. As a far-off grandson of Adam, Jesus is able to break the curse brought on by Adam's sin.

Jesus lived a perfect life. Then, as a son of Adam, he took our sin upon himself. Though he was sinless, he died in our place. But because he had no sin, the curse that began with Adam's sin was broken. After his death, Jesus rose victorious and took up the throne of his far-off grandfather David. Now, people from every nation can become children of God. Our names are written in the Book of Life and we become part of God's family tree!

READ Luke 4:1–13

The Temptation of Jesus

Imagine that warm, gooey, chocolate chip cookies are cooling on your kitchen counter. The aroma of melted chocolate fills the house. You haven't had anything to eat since lunch, and you're really hungry. But you have been told not to touch the cookies. They are for dessert, after dinner. You are alone in the kitchen. Is it hard to resist the temptation to take a cookie when no one is looking? Of course it is! (Unless you don't like warm chocolate chip cookies.) But when we disobey our parents, we are also turning away from God. Sometimes we treasure the things of this earth more than treasuring God and obeying him.

Before starting his ministry, Jesus went into the wilderness for forty days to fast and pray. Fasting meant he didn't eat any food, so he was really, really hungry. The devil tried to tempt Jesus to turn away from God the Father and obey him instead. Satan commanded Jesus to prove he was God by turning the rocks into bread. Even though Jesus was weak and very hungry, he resisted, and Satan left him.

The forty days Jesus spent in the wilderness were like the forty years Israel wandered in the wilderness after God delivered them from Egypt. After their rescue through the Red Sea, the people of Israel gave in to temptation. They complained, turned away from God to worship idols, and at the end of their journey, refused to enter the Promised Land. Jesus didn't fall for the devil's temptations, and he didn't complain when he was hungry. He worshiped God alone.

 CAPTAIN'S NOTE

Jesus said the devil is the "father of lies" and said there is "no truth in him" (John 8:44).

CAPTAIN'S CLUE

SEARCH FOR THE ANSWER IN

LUKE PART TWO: PREPARE THE WAY

CLUE:

The missing word
rhymes with pleasure.
That which I love
is "m__ t____s____".

m__ t____s____ are the next two words of the riddle.

Now let's put it together with what you have so far.

discover m__ t____s____

THE TREASURE
CHAPTER 3

A Visit from Thomas

Each day, Theos and Mira were eager to continue reading the Captain's journal. After a couple of weeks of steady reading, there came a knock (and bark) at the door.

"It's Salty!" the children shouted.

"Be right there!" said Lydia, heading to the door. She flipped the latch, opened the door, and found a very eager and excited Salty.

"Salty," said Thomas, "quiet."

"Pastor Thomas," said Lydia. "What a surprise!"

The pastor held out a basket full of carrots, lettuce, and spinach. "My garden is bursting with spinach, and it will soon go to seed in the warmer weather. I thought I'd pass along a few bags to the neighbors. I need to make room in the garden for summer crops. Time to put in the tomatoes."

"Thank you," Lydia said, taking the basket. "You are too kind. Will you join us for tea?"

"Thank you," answered Pastor Thomas.

"Please come in," she said as the two children ran to greet Salty, ignoring the pastor.

"Theos and Mira," said Lydia. "Have you forgotten your manners?"

Theos turned toward Pastor Thomas and said, "Thanks for coming!"

"Well, this can't be Theos! You're nearly as tall as me," said the pastor. Then he turned to Mira. "And, Mira! I barely recognized you!" he said. "Of course, I can't blame you both for wanting time with Salty. He certainly appreciates the attention."

Salty licked Mira. She smiled and replied, "We're glad to see both of you."

Thomas noticed the two scrolls and an old leather book on the table. He smiled, hoping the children would disclose their discovery. The kettle soon whistled, and Lydia poured the tea. "I hope you like ironwort," she said.

"Not many people know where those golden flowers grow," replied Pastor Thomas. "Nothing like a cup of mountain tea!" He paused and then continued, "So, anything new at the farm?"

Theos thought of the scrolls and lit up with excitement. "We found a clay jar by the sea with two old scrolls and a book!"

Mira picked up the scrolls, and Theos handed the journal to Pastor Thomas.

Pastor Thomas didn't let on that he had held it before. "What do we have here?" he asked.

"It's a captain's journal," Mira answered. "It's a study of these scrolls," she added, holding them up for him to see.

"The Captain's ship is called the *Providence of the Sea*," Theos added.

Then the pastor said something surprising. "You should go down to the wharf; they'll know about this ship," Pastor Thomas told the children.

"Have you heard of the *Providence*?" asked Lydia.

"The ship's history will be of interest to you," replied Pastor Thomas. "But don't look for the *Providence*; look for the *Independence*. Ask for Andros, and he'll tell you the story. He is restoring the old ship. Hoping to turn it into a museum. I'll call him to arrange a tour. While you're there, be sure to ask him to show you the lost coin. They say that doubloon offers clues that can lead to the Captain's treasure."

Theos's eyes grew wide at the word *treasure*.

"So, there is a treasure!" he shouted

"That's the legend," said Pastor Thomas. "They say the secret to finding the treasure lies with the lost coin."

"Mom, can we go?" Theos pleaded.

"Please!" Mira begged.

"If Pastor Thomas can get us a tour, we can go," said Lydia. "I'm curious as well!"

"As good as done," he replied. *The hook is set*, Pastor Thomas thought to himself as he swallowed his last sip of tea and stood up. Before Theos could ask another question, the pastor said, "Come Salty, we have more deliveries before supper."

Pastor Thomas thanked Lydia and turned toward the door. "If you encounter any questions in the journal, give me a shout," he said. Then he and Salty slipped out the door.

How did he know there were questions? wondered Theos, for the pastor hadn't even opened the journal.

• PART THREE •

The Ministry of Word and Deed

Before a sporting event, some of the players might boast that they are going to win big over their rival. It's easy to boast, but the real proof comes in performance. Some players are all talk and no action. It's easy to make a claim with your words, but much harder to follow through in action.

Luke wants his readers to know that Jesus was not all talk and no action. Luke follows Jesus's teaching with reports of his great deeds and miracles. This section starts out with Jesus saying that he is the Messiah. That is a big claim, but Jesus was more than talk. It is easy to say you will set the captive free, but we will see that Jesus followed his words with actions by setting people free from evil spirits and healing the sick. By these deeds, Jesus proved he was the Messiah, foretold by the prophets.

Truth

An axe is a tool that can cut down a mighty tree, or fashion the beams and boards needed to build a home. It can sharpen the end of a stake for a plant, or split wood for a fire. An axe can cut down or build up, sharpen, or divide. Truth works a lot like an axe. Truth can encourage good or judge evil; it can sharpen a person's thinking or divide right from wrong.

We see truth at work in the preaching of Jesus. When Jesus opened the scroll of Isaiah and read the prophet's words, he blessed everyone. When Jesus announced that the good news Isaiah promised had come, the people were amazed! Jesus was claiming that he was the promised Messiah. They asked, "Isn't this Joseph's son?" (Luke 4:22 NIV). They were amazed that such a gifted teacher could come from the house of a carpenter.

But Jesus knew their hearts were far from God. So, like an axe cuts down a tree or splits firewood, Jesus used truth to expose their hearts. Jesus reminded them that their forefathers had rejected God's prophets. As a result, God had sent the prophets Elijah and Elisha to bless non-Jews instead. When Jesus's listeners heard his words, they became enraged and tried to throw Jesus off a cliff.

 CAPTAIN'S NOTE

The words of Isaiah's prophecy were written about 700 years before Jesus was born.

Fishers of Men

Early Christians used a secret symbol to mark the places they gathered for worship—to keep them safe from arrest. A simple fish symbol, along with the Greek word for fish, let other believers know a church service was held there. The Greek letters stood for the words: Jesus, Anointed, God's Son, and Savior. They used the fish symbol, for it was said that the children of God were like fish drawn out of the water.

Four of the first disciples—two pairs of brothers—were fisherman. Peter and Andrew and James and John ran a fishing business together on the Sea of Galilee. When Jesus called them to follow him, he said, "from now on you will be catching men" (Luke 5:10).

When Jesus said, "Follow me" (Luke 5:27b), the disciples left everything to follow. Today, Jesus calls us to follow him too. We must turn from our sin and put our trust in Jesus, and believe that he died on the cross for our sin. This gospel message is like a giant net that is cast whenever it is proclaimed. Each of us who hears its call and turns from sin, is like a fish caught by the net of God's grace.

Proof of His Power

If you told your friends that you could power lift 300 pounds, they would not believe you. They would want to see it first. But if you walked over to the giant set of weights and hoisted it up off the ground above your head, you would prove that your words were true.

When a paralyzed man was lowered down through the roof by his friends, and Jesus saw their faith, Jesus said to the man, "Your sins are forgiven." The religious rulers did not believe Jesus had the power to forgive sins, so they became upset with Jesus. To prove that his words were true—that he had the power to forgive sins—Jesus ordered the lame man to rise up and walk. That was even more amazing than lifting 300 pounds!

The Pharisees left that place amazed. Still, many of them did not follow Jesus or believe he was the promised Messiah. The Pharisees thought they were righteous (good inside) and did not need forgiveness. But the truth is that we are all sinners in need of God's forgiveness. Jesus died on the cross to take the punishment we deserved. We should be like the paralyzed man and his friends, who would let nothing stop them from reaching Jesus.

Teaching with Pictures

Jesus often taught through stories and pictures. One of those pictures was of trees. He said that what grows on the outside of a tree reveals what's on the inside. So, though apple and pear trees look similar on the outside, their fruit reveals what kind of tree they are. An apple tree produces apples, and a pear tree produces pears.

Jesus said people are also like trees. Their fruit (or works) reveals what kind of person they are. Their words and actions reveal what they care most about. If their heart is filled with love for God, then praise for God will flow from their mouth. They obey and follow God's Word, and confess and repent of sin. But the person with evil desires, who loves the world more than God, refuses to confess or repent of sin.

But, before we judge others (try to remove the speck from their eye), we should judge ourselves (take the log out of our own eye). What kind of fruit is growing on your tree? Is it good fruit springing from a love for God, or bad fruit sprouting from sinful desires?

CAPTAIN'S NOTE

There is a list of good and bad fruit in Paul's letter to the Galatians.
The bad fruit, like anger and jealousy, are called the works of the flesh.
The good fruit, like love and patience, are called the fruit of the Spirit.

READ Luke 6:46–49

Building on the Rock

Did you ever build a sandcastle at low tide, and then watch the waves wash it away at high tide? A sandcastle doesn't stand a chance against the powerful waves of the ocean. When the tide comes in, the walls dissolve and fall into the sea. It is easy to see why building a house on sand is not a good idea.

Jesus said that the person who hears his teaching but does not follow it, is like one who builds their house on the sand. When the trials of life, like the wind-blown waves of a storm, crash against that house, it falls. But the person who hears the words of Jesus and follows them, is like one who builds their house on a rock. When stormy waves crash against that house, it does not fall.

Huge crowds listened to Jesus teach, but not many put his words into practice. It's easy to hear the words, "Love your enemies, do good to those who hate you" (Luke 6:27), but it is much harder to do what they say. It is easy to say you believe in Jesus, but much harder to obey his commands.

READ Luke 7:1–10

Greater Authority

Back in Jesus's day, the Romans ruled Jerusalem. A centurion could command a hundred soldiers and they would obey. But the centurion in our story sent his Jewish friends to ask Jesus for help. His servant was sick, and he had heard that Jesus healed the sick. Though he was a commander, he believed Jesus's power and authority was greater than his own.

When Jesus drew near to the centurion's home, the commander told his friends not to let Jesus inside. The Gentile centurion knew that the Jews considered him unclean. His faith was so strong that he believed Jesus only needed to say the word, and his servant would be healed.

Instead of entering the man's home, Jesus turned to the crowd and commended the centurion's faith. He said the Roman's faith was greater than any Jew of Israel. When the commander's friends returned, they found the servant healed. Matthew records a few more details, saying that Jesus didn't go to see the sick man. He simply said, "Go; let it be done for you as you have believed" (Matthew 8:13). The servant was healed at the very same moment. The centurion was right; Jesus's power was greater.

Compassion and Power

When someone dies of a contagious disease, those caring for the body wear protective clothing. This prevents any germs from spreading infection. Since ancient times, God warned his people not to touch a dead body; otherwise, they would be considered unclean for seven days (Numbers 19:11). Over those seven days, they were required to isolate from others. Naturally, people avoided touching dead bodies.

As Jesus entered the town in our Bible story, he noticed a widow crying over her dead son. Jesus felt sad for her loss and comforted her. "Don't cry," he said. He then walked over and touched the dead body. The men carrying the body immediately stopped. You can imagine their questions: Who is this? Why did he touch the body? They would soon come to understand.

Jesus, showing great power, raised the man with one word: Arise. The same power that created the universe with the words, "Let there be lights in the expanse of the heavens" (Genesis 1:14a), now raised the widow's son. The son sat up from the stretcher and spoke to his mom. The people who knew the miracles of Elijah, declared that Jesus was a prophet of God. But there was a difference between Jesus and the other prophets. Elijah raised a widow's son by calling out to God (1 Kings 17:22). Jesus, the Creator of the universe (Colossians 1:16), raised the widow's son by his own power.

CAPTAIN'S NOTE

The rule against touching a dead body did not apply to Jesus because he raised the boy from the dead! So, there was no reason for Jesus to wait seven days like the law required.

The Proof Is in the Pudding

There is an old saying: The proof is in the pudding. The true test of good pudding is not which ingredients are used, but how delicious the pudding tastes. Jesus used a similar expression, "wisdom is justified by her children" (Luke 7:35). This meant that before objecting to Jesus's actions, one should witness the fruit of his ministry.

The Pharisees didn't like what Jesus was doing—especially when he shared meals with sinners. They especially criticized him when he allowed a sinful woman to pour perfume over his feet, wipe them with her hair, and kiss them. But Jesus knew the Pharisees' thoughts and declared, "I tell you, her sins, which are many, are forgiven—for she loved much. But he who is forgiven little, loves little." And then Jesus said to her, "Your sins are forgiven" (Luke 7:47–48).

Anyone could say the words your sins are forgiven, but the proof is in the pudding. Did the people continue in their sin, or did they follow Jesus? Women like Mary Magdalene, Joanna, Susanna, and others turned from their sin and followed Jesus. They believed in Jesus and their whole lives changed. They provided for him out of their own money (Luke 8:2–3). Unlike his closest disciples, these women did not desert Jesus at his crucifixion; they stood by his side to the end, watching as he died, believing to the end (Luke 23:49).

A Light in the Darkness

What happens in your family when the power goes out during a storm? If it happens at night, the lights go out and everything is cast into darkness. You lift up your hand in front of your face, but you can't see a thing. Then a parent strikes a match to light a candle or lamp. Suddenly the whole room is lit up by that tiny flame. Once the lamp is lit and set on a table, the whole room is filled with the soft glow of the light. Now everyone can see again.

After teaching the parable of the sower, Jesus taught his disciples about light pushing back darkness. He used the example of a lantern lighting up the darkness (Luke 8:16). You see, Jesus spoke to two kinds of people. The first were those who listened carefully and put their trust in him. Their eyes were opened to the truth. Like a person standing in the light of a lamp, the parable gave them truth to see. But others rejected Jesus and his teaching. They heard the same parable, but they did not understand it (v. 11). They lived in darkness and rejected the light.

The parables hid the truth of the gospel. Only those who stayed to hear the explanation of the parable could understand its meaning. They learned that the seed in the parable is the Word of God (Luke 8:12). The Word has the power to grow in our hearts. If we receive God's Word and believe, our heart is like the fertile soil in which the seed of the gospel can sprout and grow.

READ Luke 8:22–39

Power over Life's Storms

A thunderstorm can turn a calm, sunny day into a tempest with furious wind, thunder and lightning. Imagine you are in a small boat floating on a calm sea when the storm rolls in. That's what happened to the disciples on the Sea of Galilee. As the sea began to rage, and their boat filled with water, the disciples feared for their lives. They forgot that Jesus was with them. Once awake, Jesus rebuked the storm, and the sea immediately became calm.

This story is in our Bible to display Jesus's power, and to encourage us to trust him through life's storms. Few of us will ever meet a tempest on the sea, but we will all face trials. Losing a loved one, experiencing sickness, or facing a challenge at school are examples of the kind of storms we might face in life. We need to remember that our all-powerful Jesus is with us when troubles come. We can call to him in prayer, for he has the power to

calm the wind and the waves of the storms in our lives.

When Jesus and the disciples landed their boat, they faced another storm: a man tormented by a tempest of evil from demons. As he came toward Jesus for help, the demons cried out in fear. Jesus commanded the spirits to leave, and in minutes, the darkness of evil fled. The man stood liberated in light. His storm had ended. Like the disciples in the boat during the squall, the man need not have feared, for Jesus was near.

The Bible tells us that God will never leave or forsake those who trust in him (Deuteronomy 31:6; Hebrews 13:5). Always remember, Jesus remains ready to rebuke the wind and the waves. We need not fear when life's troubles blow in like a storm, for he is with us.

CAPTAIN'S NOTE

Peter later taught that God uses the trials of our lives to test our faith and make us pure like gold refined in a fire (1 Peter 1:6-7).

Power over Sickness and Death

Have you ever needed to ask for help? Maybe you're trying to reach a heavy glass pitcher on a tall shelf. You pull up a chair and stand on your tiptoes, but you still can't reach it. You're simply not tall enough. Then your mom comes along and you ask for help. She smiles and gladly lifts the pitcher with little effort. She has the power to do what you could not.

In our story, Jesus was on his way to heal a twelve-year-old girl who was dying. As he walked to the girl's house, Jesus encountered a woman who was sick. Though she had given all her money to doctors, she was still ill. No one had been able to heal her. But Jesus could do what no one else could. The woman saw Jesus and believed that all she needed to do was touch him. As soon as she did, she was instantly healed.

Just then, a messenger from the sick girl's family arrived with the sad news that Jesus didn't have to come because the girl had died. Even though it was impossible to heal her, Jesus was not alarmed. He said, "Do not fear; only believe, and she will be well" (Luke 8:50). When Jesus arrived at the girl's house, he declared that the girl was only sleeping. The people laughed, for they knew she had died. But Jesus went to her, took her by the hand and said, "Child, arise" (v. 54). At once, she got up out of bed, alive. Jesus proved that his power was greater than sickness or death.

Power to Create

Bakers mix yeast, flour, and water to make bread. After the dough is mixed, it is set aside to rise. As the yeast goes to work, it feeds on the sugars in flour, and releases gas bubbles that cause the dough to expand. A little bit of yeast can cause the ball of dough to multiply and fill an entire bowl. But it would take more than a little yeast to multiply five loaves into enough bread to feed a crowd of five thousand. Only God's power could do that!

So far in Luke's gospel, we see that Jesus had power over the storm at sea and over the storm in the man with demons. He healed the sick and raised the dead and now, he feeds five thousand people gathered to hear his teaching. Jesus uses his power to create. He takes five loaves and two fish and multiplies them to feed the thousands of people gathered on the hillside. To prove that Jesus created more fish and loaves than he started with, Luke adds an important detail: When all were finished eating, twelve basketfuls of pieces of bread and fish remained. Even just one of those baskets contained more food than Jesus started with.

The apostle Paul taught the Colossians about Jesus being the Creator. He said, "by him all things were created, in heaven and on earth, visible and invisible, whether thrones or dominions or rulers or authorities—all things were created through him and for him" (Colossians 1:16). If Jesus could create the whole earth with words, multiplying food was certainly something he could do.

Who Am I?

Did you ever play the guessing game, Who am I? One person pretends to be someone else. The rest of the group takes turns asking questions to try and figure out who they are. Imagine you are playing the game and pretending to be George Washington. If someone asks, "Are you a leader?" You would answer yes. Someone else might ask, "Are you a president?" Again the answer is yes. The game goes on until someone gets to the correct answer, asking, "Are you George Washington?"

After demonstrating his power, Jesus, in a sense, played Who Am I? with his disciples. He asked them, "Who do the crowds say that

I am?" None of the disciples' answers were correct. Then Jesus asked again, "Who do you say that I am?" Peter answered, "The Christ of God." Christ means God's Anointed One— the chosen son of Adam, promised to end the curse of sin. Peter must have felt proud to answer correctly.

In Matthew's gospel, we learn that Peter had help in getting the correct answer. Jesus told him, "Blessed are you, Simon Bar-Jonah! For flesh and blood has not revealed this to you, but my Father who is in heaven" (Matthew 16:17). It's not cheating if God gives you the right answer!

CAPTAIN'S NOTE *The Old Testament is full of prophecies foretelling the coming of a promised Son of David. Read 2 Samuel 7:12-13; Isaiah 42:1; and Daniel 7:13-14.*

The Transfiguration

When you run electricity through a light bulb, a thin wire inside transforms. The wire filament lights up with power. Each time you flip a light switch in your home, a light bulb transfigures before your very eyes. *Transfigure* is a word used to describe a tremendous change—one that often reveals power or glory.

The power and glory of Jesus is far greater than a light bulb. When Jesus took Peter, James, and John up the mountain, he allowed them to see his power and glory as he transfigured before them. Later Peter described himself and his friends as eyewitnesses of Jesus's majesty (2 Peter 1:16).

Jesus demonstrated his power over creation, sickness, and even demon-possession. To three of his disciples, he revealed his power and glory. While shining with brilliant light, God the Father spoke to the disciples saying, "This is my Son, my Chosen One; listen to him!" (Luke 9:35b). As we read the story of Jesus's transfiguration, God calls us to obey that same command—to listen to Jesus and believe.

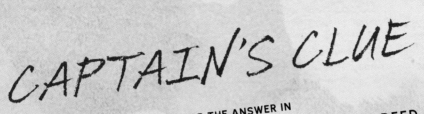

CAPTAIN'S CLUE

SEARCH FOR THE ANSWER IN

LUKE PART THREE: THE MINISTRY OF WORD AND DEED

CLUE:

He opened the scroll
and looked for the place
where it was wr _ _ _ _ _n,
the news of God's grace.

wr_ _ _ _ _n is the next part of the riddle.

Now let's put it together with what you have so far.

discover my treasure wr _ _ _ _n

CHAPTER 4

The Independence

The smell of fish and burning oil greeted Theos, Mira, and Lydia as they stepped off the bus and onto the parking lot near the Naxos main dock. Their bus pulled away, revealing a view of the sea. Hundreds of sailboats were tied along slips lining the harbor, with masts like giant toothpicks poking up from a party tray. There, among the smaller sailboats, stood a massive clipper ship moored to a long pier jutting out to the sea. A web of ropes and rigging hung from two tall masts. With each step Theos, Mira, and Lydia took, the ship grew taller. As they neared the dock, Mira noticed the worn gilded letters on the boat. "*Independence*", she read.

"This is it," said Lydia. "This is the Captain's trading ship." Up ahead, a gangway led from the ship to the dock. A hand-painted sandwich board stood on the cement pier next to a wooden ticket booth. Theos read aloud the freshly-painted words: "The Providence of the Sea. Five Drachmae for adults. Three Drachmae for children. Children three and under free."

Andros called down from the ship, "Ahoy, mates! Welcome aboard the *Providence*. Come on up the gangway," he shouted with a smile and a wave. Once aboard the ship, Lydia reached into her bag for a twenty drachmae note.

"No need to pay; it's on the house," Andros said.

"Really?" Lydia asked.

"Yes, ma'am. Orders from headquarters. Pastor Thomas said to give you all the VIP tour—complimentary." Andros pointed to a gray strip of paint on a tattered shirt. We're painting today. So, mind the signs. We open a week from Friday. Pastor Thomas said he wished he could join you for the tour, but he left earlier this morning for a couple weeks. He's attending the annual pastor's conference in the UK and visiting friends."

"How do you know Pastor Thomas?" asked Lydia.

"Why he's the one who hired me to restore her," he said as he slapped his hand on the ship's railing. "Follow me."

To Lydia, the ship felt mysterious.

While walking briskly to keep up, Theos asked, "Why does the ship have two names?"

"That is a good question! I'll tell you about that in a little while. Down you go," he said, opening a door. "We'll begin the tour below deck in the cargo hold."

After a steep descent into the hold of the ship, Andros offered a brief history.

"Apollos Adamos commissioned the building of the *Providence of the Sea* in 1860.

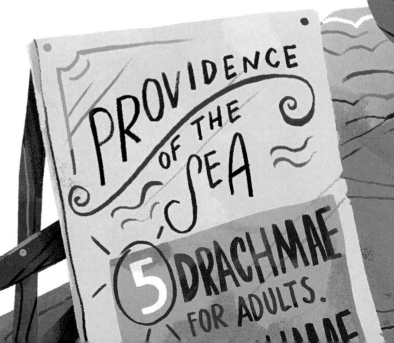

"Apollos owned and operated a large wooden pier here. He loaded the hull of the *Providence* with emery and marble mined in Naxos. The ship traveled north to Spain and south as far as the Ivory Coast of Africa, selling the marble and emery and returning with gum, indigo, ivory, and gold. There was good money in the emery trade.

"Apollos had two sons. The older one was named Philip, and the younger, Theophilus. As the two boys grew, Apollos planned for them to take over the family business. Philip was keen with numbers, but Theophilus loved the sea. Apollos bought Theophilus a small sailboat for his twelfth birthday. While Philip helped his father, Theophilus went sailing. He was a rebel at heart. He hated the idea of sitting at a desk, counting bills of lading. By sixteen, the lad had circled our island on his own, proving his seafaring skills. He wanted to captain a ship of his own, but Apollos knew he wasn't ready.

"But when Theophilus turned twenty, he demanded the *Providence* as his inheritance. Reluctantly, Apollos agreed, and Theophilus left Naxos with a hull full of cargo. He all but stole the ship. Once in Spain, he promptly sold the ship's cargo and changed its name from the *Providence* to the *Independence*.

"Theophilus sailed from Spain to Africa and back again, didn't return home, and never married. They say he was married to the sea. Over the years, Theophilus amassed a fortune in gold, sailing back and forth from Spain to Africa. Rumor has it that the treasure is hidden somewhere along the coast of Naxos. "

"What about the lost coin?" Theos asked.

"Ah, yes. They say that it is the key to finding the treasure. Before we are through, I'll give you a peek. We found the lost coin when we swept the Captain's quarters. It is on display on the cabin wall, where we'll end our tour."

Theos could hardly wait.

PART FOUR

The Journey to the Cross

Up until now, Luke's story of the life of Christ has retold the accounts of Jesus spreading the good news through powerful signs. As Jesus healed the sick, calmed the storm, and set people free from enemies, many believed. In this next section of his gospel, Luke includes parables not found in the other gospels, for example, the good Samaritan, the lost coin, and the parable of the prodigal son. Also, the emphasis shifts. As Jesus drew nearer to the cross, his focus turned toward his disciples. Luke records Jesus's warning, "Let these words sink into your ears: The Son of Man is about to be delivered into the hands of men" (Luke 9:44).

Though the disciples did not understand what Jesus meant by those words, Jesus knew the road leading to the cross was close at hand. His arrest, trial, and crucifixion were not far away. Jesus did not shrink back from his mission to save us. Luke tells us, "When the days drew near for him to be taken up, he set his face to go to Jerusalem" (Luke 9:51). Those words of Luke mark the transition in the life of Jesus. As you read this section, keep in mind that Jesus knew his future and gladly gave up his life for us. The writer of Hebrews gives us a window into the heart of Christ in this description: "who for the joy that was set before him endured the cross, despising the shame" (Hebrews 12:2).

On to Jerusalem

There comes a point when the preparation is complete and a mountain climber must begin the climb. They collect their equipment. They study the route to the top and map out the risks. They know they will face danger and difficulties. But still, if they are going to get to the top, they must begin their climb.

Jesus faced a climb—to a hill called Golgotha. Jesus knew his journey was leading to his death. Jesus offered this warning to his disciples: "Let these words sink into your ears: The Son of Man is about to be delivered into the hands of men" (Luke 9:44). The disciples didn't understand that Jesus was predicting his own arrest. Sadly, they spent time arguing about which of them was the greatest (v. 46). They likely believed Jesus would use his power to defend himself. If he could command the wind and the waves, surely he could win any battle.

Jesus was gracious toward the disciples, ultimately trusting God's plan. The prophets rightly foretold that he would be led like a lamb to his death and not resist (Isaiah 53:7). So, Jesus "set his face to go to Jerusalem" (Luke 9:51b). Jesus had not come to deliver them from Rome, but to set his people free from sin and death, by taking the punishment they deserve upon himself.

CAPTAIN'S NOTE

While the cross meant great suffering for Jesus, it also brought him joy, for he knew that his death and resurrection opened a way for all of God's children to enter heaven. Read Hebrews 12:2.

Two by Two

Jesus sent seventy-two of his disciples out in pairs to spread the good news of the gospel to the surrounding villages. Solomon said, "Two are better than one, because they have a good return for their labor: If either of them falls down, one can help the other up" (Ecclesiastes 4:9–10a NIV). Jesus said, "I am sending you out as lambs in the midst of wolves" (Luke 10:3). He also told them to leave their money, and extra clothes and sandals behind. He wanted them to trust God—but he didn't leave them alone; he sent them out in pairs.

The disciples returned from this scary mission with great joy. They obeyed Jesus and discovered that even the demons were no match for them. For when they commanded them to come out of a person in Jesus's name, the demons fled. Jesus was glad for his disciples' success but told them, "Do not rejoice in this, that the spirits are subject to you, but rejoice that your names are written in heaven" (Luke 10:20).

This is an amazing truth for us to remember. All those who believe and follow Jesus should rejoice, knowing their names are also written in the book of life forever (Revelation 20:15).

CAPTAIN'S NOTE

Everyone who trusts in Jesus has their name written in the Book of Life. Their names will remain there for all eternity. God has promised it, and he never breaks his promises.

Love Your Neighbor

One loving thing we can do for our family is to take out the trash. Removing a stinky trash can is a blessing to everyone. But often, we just keep adding more trash, hoping someone else will empty it. Perhaps we don't want to get dirty. But when a servant sees a need, they meet it. This is an act of love.

Jesus told the parable of the good Samaritan to show us how to love those around us. In the parable, no one from Israel (God's people) stopped to help an injured man. What if the injured man soon died? If they touched a dead body, they would become unclean. But Jesus wanted to show how selfish they were. So, Jesus brought a Samaritan into his story—a person the Jews looked down on. It is only the Samaritan, a non-Jew, who showed mercy and stopped to help the injured man. The idea that Samaritans and Jews should be neighbors, would have shocked the crowd and revealed their selfishness.

Jesus loved and served others. On the cross, he took our sin and died to show his love for God and others. So, the next time you see a full trash can, remember his example. Choose to walk in love, as Jesus did and continues to do for us.

CAPTAIN'S NOTE The Samaritans were only half Jewish. They came from the ten tribes of Israel that split off from King Rehoboam. When they traveled north to the land of Samaria, they intermarried with non-Jewish idol worshipers. This explains why the Jews looked down on them.

Mary and Martha

Imagine you have been asked to do the dishes. As you stand at the sink, everyone piles their dishes beside you and leaves. You wonder, *Why do I have to stay and do the dishes alone? Why isn't anyone helping?*

That's how Martha felt in our story. She had been preparing and serving food while her sister, Mary, had been listening to Jesus. No one seemed to care that she alone had been doing all the work. Finally, Martha complained to Jesus, "Do you not care that my sister has left me to serve alone? Tell her then to help me" (Luke 10:40b). Jesus corrected Martha, for she had missed an opportunity to spend time with him. He said, "Mary has chosen what is better, and it will not be taken away from her" (v. 42 NIV).

Later, at Lazarus's death, Martha did not repeat the same mistake. Instead, she ran to Jesus for help saying, "Lord, if you had been here, my brother would not have died. But even now I know that whatever you ask from God, God will give you" (John 11:21–22). Jesus replied, "I am the resurrection and the life. Whoever believes in me, though he die, yet shall he live" (v. 25). Then Jesus asked, "Do you believe this?" Martha replied yes, and then Jesus, in his great power, raised her brother from the dead.

Today, Jesus calls us to draw near to him like Mary and Martha. We get to know Jesus better by spending time with him—by reading our Bibles and talking to him. Then we find rest and peace knowing he is the one who can forgive our sin and change our lives.

The Lord's Prayer

A scorpion has eight legs with crab-like claws on the front and a tail with a stinger on the back. Scorpions are fierce hunters. They grab their prey with their claws and thrust their tail down to sting. Jesus used the example of a scorpion and snake to help us realize how eager God is to answer our prayers. When we cry out to him for help, he doesn't trick us by giving us a scorpion. Instead, he responds with love.

After the disciples heard Jesus pray, they asked him to teach them how to pray. Jesus answered by teaching them the Lord's Prayer—a prayer to God as their Father in heaven. Praying to God is like asking for a parent's help. The Lord's Prayer teaches us to ask God, our heavenly Father, for our daily needs—to help us love others and to strengthen us against sin.

Another way to pray is to thank God for how he answers prayer. The Lord's Prayer begins, "Father, hallowed be your name" and "your kingdom come" (Luke 11:2b). God's kingdom is his loving, mighty rule over all things. When we pray, "your kingdom come," we welcome God's rule over our hearts and lives.

On the Inside

Would you ever drink from a cup that was clean on the outside but filthy on the inside? Jesus uses this example to warn the Pharisees. They want to look good on the outside, while filled with sin on the inside. But Jesus knows their hearts and speaks strongly against them.

We too can be like the Pharisees. We can try our best to look good on the outside, but inside our hearts we can hold anger, unforgiveness, bitterness, and jealousy. Today's Bible passage encourages us to be clean on the inside. We can turn from our sin, confess it to God, and receive his forgiveness. (Remember the Lord's Prayer.) If we have sinned against someone else, we can seek their forgiveness too.

Sadly, many of the Pharisees did not turn away from their sins or ask God to forgive them. Instead of repenting (turning from their sin), they sought a way to trap Jesus (Luke 11:54).

CAPTAIN'S NOTE

People often judge others by what they see on the outside—in their appearance and actions. God told Samuel that man looks on the outside, but God looks at the heart. Read 1 Samuel 16:7

A Word about Money

Gold is the purest form of money. We first see it mentioned in Genesis 13 where Abram was "rich in gold." Gold is valuable because it is rare. If you melted down all the gold ever discovered in the whole world, it would fit into one, Olympic-sized swimming pool. Gold coins have been used for hundreds of years as a way to buy the things you need. This has led people to believe that money can solve all their problems.

In today's reading, a man in the crowd asked Jesus to tell his brother to give him half of his inheritance. An inheritance is money or property passed down from one's parents to their children. The man surely thought money would solve his problems. But Jesus wanted the crowd to understand that it is God who meets your needs.

Jesus made it clear: If God provides food for the birds and flowers, how much more will he provide for our needs? Instead of seeking after money, Jesus said to "seek his kingdom" (Luke 12:31). Seeking his kingdom means welcoming God's rule over your life. As we consider him in all things, we can trust that God will provide everything we need—food, clothing, and shelter. So, we don't have to worry. He will always take care of us.

Be Ready

Figs are very sweet and are often baked in cookies. But not all fig trees bear this sweet fruit. Some fig trees grow tall and bushy and use their energy to make leaves instead of fruit. Fig growers know you must pinch off new growth to help form new fruit. Yet even with pruning and care, some fig trees never bear fruit; they only make leaves. If a fig tree does not bear fruit, it must be cut down. That is the example Jesus used to teach us that we also must bear fruit. When we turn from sin and live for Jesus, he (the gardener) sees our fruit.

Jesus also used the example of a master who goes away to attend a wedding. We are like the servants, who need to be ready and waiting for their master's return. So how do we prepare for his return? We need to believe and trust in Jesus. Then, when our master, Jesus, returns, he will bless us with a banquet (heaven).

Those who believe and trust in Jesus are like the fig tree that bears fruit. Our fruit is the good works that sprout from following Jesus and obeying his teaching. As we live for him, we joyfully anticipate his return, for we don't know when it will be (Luke 12:40).

Healing on the Sabbath

The Pharisees made up all kinds of rules to ensure that people didn't work on the Sabbath. They made a long list of thirty-nine different types of work that were absolutely forbidden. They hoped their rules would save them. One rule said that you could not carry any weight, write things down, or even draw a picture on the Sabbath. (Can you imagine not being able to do these things one day each week?) One type of work the Jewish law did allow for on the Sabbath was the care of animals and living things. For example, a donkey could be untied and led to food and water.

On one particular Sabbath, Jesus healed a disabled woman. Rather than rejoice at the miracle, the ruler of the synagogue became angry and complained that Jesus was working on the Sabbath. He told everyone that it was wrong for Jesus to heal the woman. Jesus rebuked the man, reminding him of the rule about animals. He asked, "How could I care for a donkey, but not one of God's children?" Jesus continued, "Ought not this woman, a daughter of Abraham whom Satan bound for eighteen years, be loosed from this bond on the Sabbath day?" (Luke 13:16).

Jesus called the ruler a hypocrite (v. 15). He looked good on the outside, following all his manmade rules. But he refused to rejoice when the woman was healed. Instead of putting his trust in Jesus, he opposed him.

The Narrow Door

Did you ever go to a store to buy something, but arrive just after it has closed? You knock on the door because you see the employees inside. But they point to the closed sign. Then they point to their watch and say, "We are closed!" Thankfully, you can always return to the store tomorrow.

In today's passage, we learn that there's a window of time for us to turn to Jesus. One day, that window will close. Each person has an opportunity to believe in Jesus while they are alive. But some people think they have plenty of time. They can live however they want here on earth. They forget that we will not live forever. Once you die, the door to heaven closes and you can no longer turn away from your sin to believe. It will be too late.

Jesus said that the doorway to heaven is narrow. Matthew records a similar teaching: "Enter by the narrow gate. For the gate is wide and the way is easy that leads to destruction, and those who enter by it are many. For the gate is narrow and the way is hard that leads to life, and those who find it are few" (Matthew 7:13–14). The good news is that the way is still open for us to call out to God in faith. The sign on the door says Open.

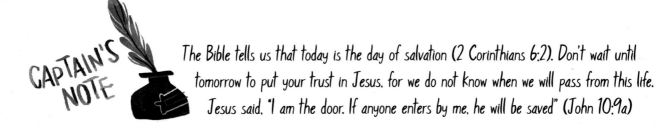

CAPTAIN'S NOTE The Bible tells us that today is the day of salvation (2 Corinthians 6:2). Don't wait until tomorrow to put your trust in Jesus, for we do not know when we will pass from this life. Jesus said, "I am the door. If anyone enters by me, he will be saved" (John 10:9a)

The Banquet

When two people are engaged to be married, they send out invitations to their wedding. Family and friends look forward to attending their wedding. But there are always some people who cannot make it and must decline. When this happens, more invitations are sent out to fill every seat.

In today's parable, Jesus used the illustration of a great banquet. Believing in Jesus is like saying "yes" to the invitation. Jesus came to the Jews and invited them to believe. Sadly, many, like the religious rulers and teachers, refused. They rejected Jesus. So, Jesus expanded his invitation. He called the sinners, the sick, the tax collectors, and he also welcomed the Samaritans, like the woman at the well (John 4:7). One day, all those who turned from their sin to trust in Jesus, will join in a heavenly wedding banquet feast (Revelation 19:9).

Today, his invitation to the banquet goes out to me and to you. The question for us is: Will we trust in Jesus for the forgiveness of our sins? If we turn from our sin and say "yes" to Jesus, we will be welcomed into heaven and join the banquet. Jesus longs for all people to join him on that day.

The Lost Sheep and Lost Coin

Did you ever lose something special and go on a wild search to find it? Everyone in your house starts looking. Upstairs and downstairs. In closets and under beds. When you finally find the special missing item, everyone celebrates!

Jesus used two parables, the lost sheep and the lost coin, to help people understand how God searches for his lost children to bring them home. The Bible teaches that we are lost sinners and that Jesus has come to find us (Luke 19:10). Did you know that God is looking for you? Once we understand that we are lost in our sin, we realize that we can call on Jesus for help. Just as we rejoice when we find our missing item, Jesus celebrates when he rescues us.

We can be sure that Jesus will find all his lost sheep. He promised, "this is the will of him who sent me, that I should lose nothing of all that he has given me, but raise it up on the last day. For this is the will of my Father, that everyone who looks on the Son and believes in him should have eternal life, and I will raise him up on the last day" (John 6:39–40).

CAPTAIN'S NOTE

I got the idea to hide the location of my treasure from the parable of the lost coin. Keep reading, my friend, and you might find it! I cut the secret into a Spanish doubloon. Made of 18 carat gold, it's the treasure of great pirates like Blackbeard and Calico Jack. Stay the course and it could be yours!

The Lost Sons

A carpenter calls a wooden plank that's longer than the others "proud" because it sticks out. The word *proud* means lifted up. A person is proud when they think they are better than someone else. The Bible speaks against pride. God calls us to live humbly and says that he "opposes the proud but gives grace to the humble" (James 4:6). God allows trials in our lives that expose our pride and humble us. Solomon warned, "Pride goes before destruction, and a haughty spirit before a fall" (Proverbs 16:18).

There are two sons in our parable, both were proud. The younger son demanded his father give him his share of his wealth, something he wasn't supposed to receive until his father died. Everyone could see the pride and disrespect in his demand. After the father gave him the money, the younger son left and spent it foolishly. When his money ran out and he had nothing to eat, he realized his error. He humbled himself and returned to his father.

The older son was also proud. Although he served his father, he became proud of his own works. His hidden pride was exposed when his father welcomed the younger son home and called for a feast to celebrate. The older son refused his father's request to join the party. He felt he was the one who deserved a banquet, not his younger brother. His pride led him to dishonor his father just as his brother had.

CAPTAIN'S NOTE

Beware of pride. Paul taught, "Do not think of yourself more highly than you ought" (Romans 12:3 NIV). "Rather, in humility value others above yourselves" (Philippians 2:3b NIV).

You Can't Serve Both God and Money

A bowling ball has three fingerholes to make it easy to pick up and roll. Because bowling balls are large and heavy, you can only hold one in your hand at a time. A bowler must choose a single ball to roll down the alley to knock down the pins. It is impossible to roll two balls with the same hand.

It is also impossible to serve both God and money. Jesus explained it like this: "No servant can serve two masters, for either he will hate the one and love the other, or he will be devoted to the one and despise the other. You cannot serve God and money" (Luke 16:13). Just like you can only hold one bowling ball in your hand at a time, you can only hold one first love in your heart. God wants us to make him our first love.

The Greek word for money is *mammon*. Mammon refers to any kind of riches—including money we earn, or toys we buy, or items we receive as gifts. They all count as riches. And the Bible is clear that we can't serve God and things. He wants to be our only master. He wants to be our first love. Do you love things—electronics or clothes or sports—more than God?

The Rich Man and Lazarus

Warning signs alert people to danger. Signs can prevent us from going down a dangerous path. When a bridge is washed out by a storm, for example, the police block off the road. Then they post warning signs to keep us safe.

The parable of Lazarus is like a warning sign, alerting us to trouble. It's in the Bible to show us a better path than that of the rich man. The rich man lived his life for himself. He loved his riches but did not love or worship God. (Remember that you cannot serve both God and money.) This led him down a dangerous path. After he died, it was too late to turn back or change. Solomon warns against this danger by sharing the same proverb twice: "There is a way that seems right to a man, but its end is the way to death" (Proverbs 14:12; 16:25).

The warning sign for us is clear: Turn away from sin and live for God while you are alive. Peter urged the people to turn from their sin and believe in Jesus when he said: "Repent therefore, and turn back, that your sins may be blotted out" (Acts 3:19). God posts these warnings out of love for us. He wants the very best for us. He wants to lead us down the best path.

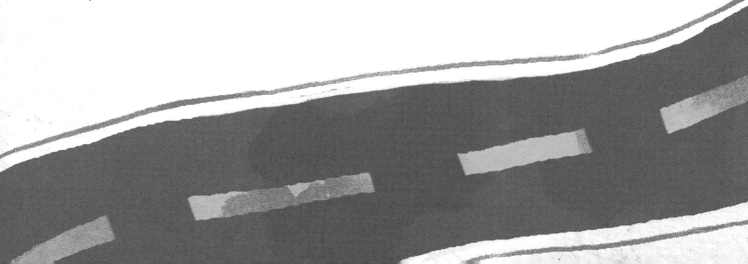

CAPTAIN'S NOTE

Jesus really did bring a man named Lazarus back from the grave (John 11:43-44). Even when they saw Jesus raise a man from the dead, some of the Jews still did not believe, but instead planned to kill Jesus (v. 53).

Forgiveness and a Mustard Seed of Faith

A mustard seed is tiny compared with a sunflower seed. It is super tiny compared with an acorn or coconut, both of which are also seeds. Jesus used the picture of the tiny mustard seed to make his point. If we have faith as tiny as a mustard seed, we can find the faith to forgive those who sin against us.

Jesus told the disciples that even if a person sins seven times in the same day and repents, they should offer that person forgiveness. Imagine your younger sibling scribbling on your notebook seven times in the same day! The disciples thought Jesus was asking too much. They said, "Increase our faith!" (Luke 17:5). Jesus then used the example of the mustard seed, saying that with only a little bit of faith, they could move a mulberry tree by their command. In other words, he was saying that even the smallest bit of faith in God is enough to help us forgive others.

The apostle Paul taught the Ephesians how to find faith to forgive. He said, "Be kind to one another, tenderhearted, forgiving one another, as God in Christ forgave you" (Ephesians 4:32). We find the faith to forgive by remembering how Jesus first forgave us. We sin all the time, and yet if we confess our sins to God, and place our trust in Jesus, God forgives all our sins. So, remembering what Jesus did for us on the cross, even just a small mustard seed's worth, will help us forgive others when they sin against us. Even if they sin against us again and again.

Ten Lepers

There is a four-word question parents often use to prompt their children to say thank you. The four-word question is: What do you say? If you stop by a neighbor's house for a visit on a hot day and they offer you an ice cream treat, your parent might whisper in your ear, "What do you say?" That's your cue to say thank you.

Ten lepers cried out to Jesus for healing. All ten obeyed Jesus's call to go to the priest who could declare them "clean" and then send them home. All ten were healed as they obeyed Jesus. But, only one leper returned to thank him.

The leper who returned received a greater blessing. Jesus commended him for his faith. The apostle Paul said, "For by grace you have been saved through faith. And this is not your own doing; it is the gift of God, not a result of works, so that no one may boast" (Ephesians 2:8–9). Ten lepers were healed, but only the one was commended for his faith. We don't know if the others put their faith in Jesus or not. The Bible tells us that God makes the sun rise on evil and good (Matthew 5:45), but only those who trust in the Lord by faith will be saved (Ephesians 2:8).

Come Like a Child

Young children trust their parents to help them do things like cross a busy street or carry them across a stream. Children are full of curiosity and questions. They want to know what everything is and how it works. And they typically trust what they are told.

In today's story, two men were praying in the temple, but only one of the men trusted God. The tax collector humbled himself and trusted God, but the Pharisee trusted in his own good works (Luke 18:12). The tax collector recognized he was a sinner, and he trusted God to save him.

Jesus said, "Whoever does not receive the kingdom of God like a child shall not enter it" (Luke 18:17). Matthew records these words, "unless you turn and become like children, you will never enter the kingdom of heaven. Whoever humbles himself like this child is the greatest in the kingdom of heaven" (Matthew 18:3–4). None of us can earn our way to heaven by our works, but if we come to Jesus with childlike faith, we can be forgiven and welcomed into the kingdom of heaven.

Zacchaeus

Have you ever climbed a ladder to reach an attic, or used a stepstool to reach a tall shelf? In today's story, Zacchaeus, too short to see over the crowd, climbed a tree so he could see Jesus.

Zacchaeus was a tax collector. Tax collectors were typically disliked for cheating people out of money. They forced people to pay more money than they actually owed. They then kept the extra money for themselves.

But Zacchaeus was a tax collector who was drawn to Jesus. When he heard that Jesus had come to town, he climbed a tree to see him. And it just so happened that Jesus was also looking for Zacchaeus.

Jesus went right up to Zacchaeus and invited himself to dinner (Luke 19:5). Even though Zacchaeus was a sinner, Jesus loved him. Zacchaeus's whole life changed that day. He turned from sin, and said he would pay back all the money he had stolen from others. He also said he would give half his money to the poor. Jesus came to rescue Zacchaeus. He came to "seek and save the lost" (Luke 19:10).

Did you know that Jesus is still seeking and saving the lost today? Will you, like Zacchaeus, turn from a life of sin and trust in Jesus?

CAPTAIN'S NOTE

The prophet Jeremiah gave Israel a message from God—that if we seek after God with all our heart, we will find him. "I will be found by you, declares the LORD." (Jeremiah 29:14a).

The Triumphal Entry

Can you imagine what it would be like to see a bunch of rocks come to life? That is the picture Jesus used to teach the Pharisees. When the Pharisees complained to Jesus about the disciples worshiping him, Jesus replied, "I tell you, if these were silent, the very stones would cry out" (Luke 19:40).

Five hundred years before Jesus was born, the prophet Zechariah foretold, "Rejoice greatly, O daughter of Zion! Shout aloud, O daughter of Jerusalem! Behold, your king is coming to you; righteous and having salvation is he, humble and mounted on a donkey, on a colt, the foal of a donkey" (Zechariah 9:9). Jesus fulfilled this prophecy the day he rode into Jerusalem.

Many of the Jews knew Zechariah's prophecy and gathered to welcome Jesus. They watched him heal the sick and raise the dead. They believed he was the promised king. When they saw Jesus riding on a donkey, they shouted Zechariah's words by calling Jesus "King." Sadly, it was the Jewish people, stirred up by the Pharisees, who shouted several days later, "Crucify him." They feared losing their power over people, so they rejected Jesus. Even worse, they called for his death.

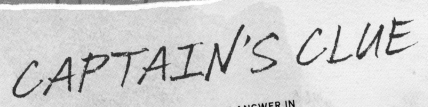

CAPTAIN'S CLUE

SEARCH FOR THE ANSWER IN

LUKE PART FOUR: THE JOURNEY TO THE CROSS

CLUE:

The rulers objected;
said, they may not shout.
But if they stayed quiet
the st __ n __ would cry out.

Now add the word in to the missing word above.

in st __ n __ is the next part of the riddle.

Now let's put it together with what you have so far.

discover my treasure written
in st __ n __

CHAPTER 5

The Doubloon

And now, the moment you have been waiting for . . . the Captain's quarters!" Andros declared as he led the family through a narrow hall. Just ahead stood a heavy wooden door, slightly ajar, with a sign that read, "Caution: Wet Paint."

They all slipped through the opening, careful to avoid the fresh paint. Once inside, Andros drew attention to the far wall.

"There it is," he said, pointing to the coin.

"It's a gold doubloon. I mounted it upon the ship's plaque and covered it with plate glass for protection."

Theos stared at the coin. Three holes were cut into it. Before he could ask about them, Andros continued. "You might have noticed the holes. At the very top is the outline of Mt. Zeus. Below it, is a cross and a star-shaped hole. They say if you hold the coin up to the afternoon light, and match the outline to Mt. Zeus, the star will lead you to the Captain's treasure."

Mira read the plaque aloud:

*Providence is
the secret hand of God which works upon the earth
to move all things in keeping with his will.
From the flicker of a sparrow's wing
to the drip of a single raindrop on a distant hill,
all unfold as the Lord intends.
There is no luck, no accident, nor random chance.
Every detail of life is woven by God's hand
into the tapestry of his plan for the good of his children.
So is the course of this ship, the Providence,
led upon the sea.*

Apollos Adamos

Looking closely at the plaque, Theos did his best to remember the pattern of the holes. If only he could borrow the doubloon for a day, he was sure he could find the treasure.

Andros explained, "Though Theophilus renamed his father's ship the *Independence*, he left this plaque alone." Andros then proceeded to tell almost exactly the same story the children had read in the Captain's journal.

"Twenty-five years later, Theophilus gave free passage to a missionary named Cristobal, to a place called Naxos. The missionary, along with his wife and son Thomas, were traveling back from work in Africa. Each night upon the ship, Cristobal read from two Bible scrolls: the books of Luke and Acts. On one of those nights, God touched Theophilus's heart, and he believed. When the ship reached Naxos,

Cristobal gave Theophilus the two Bible scrolls as a parting gift. At least that is what Pastor Thomas told me. He was only a boy back then, but he remembers the journey well."

When they heard the word scrolls, Theos and Mira exchanged excited glances. Theos and Mira said nothing, but were eager to discuss the coin's connection with Pastor Thomas.

Andros continued, "It was the first time Theophilus had returned home in many years, but his father had always been waiting. Nearly every hour of every day, Apollos scanned the sea for the return of his son. Twenty-five years later, Apollos was the first to spot the *Providence* in the bay. He immediately rushed to the pier.

"Theophilus hugged his father tightly and tearfully repented. Adamos forgave

Theophilus and welcomed him with great joy. Theophilus rejoined the family business, but as for the *Providence*, she never sailed again.

"It was a good thing Theophilus returned when he did. A year later, a bucket of oily rags burst into flames. Within minutes, the fire raged out of control and burned the whole pier down to the waterline. Theophilus ran for his father and pulled him from the flames. But not soon enough. Apollos had breathed in too much smoke and passed into glory later that evening. The family business was lost, but the *Providence*, anchored off shore, survived. There is more to the story, but Pastor Thomas said he would fill in the gaps.

"Well, that is the end of the tour," said Andros abruptly. "I'll show you back to the gangway."

"Thank you," Lydia replied, her mind swirling with questions. She was eager to speak with Pastor Thomas.

The family followed Andros back to the gangway and said goodbye. Just before they reached the pier, Andros called out to them.

"Wait!" he shouted. "I almost forgot!" He reached into his right pocket and retrieved two coins. "We've made souvenir replicas of the lost coin. Pastor Thomas wanted you to have the first ones." He handed a coin to Theos and another to Mira. "Hold on to these. In a few short weeks, after we open, hundreds of these coins will be traveling the island with everyone searching for the Captain's treasure."

Theos couldn't believe his luck. Now he was sure to find the treasure!

• PART FIVE •

The Death and Victory of Christ

This is the last section of Luke's gospel. Within these closing chapters, Jesus is put on trial, found guilty, and crucified. Then, in a great demonstration of power, Jesus rises from the dead on the third day.

We see three themes in this last section of the book of Luke. First, we learn that Jesus is aware of all that is about to take place. He knows he is going to the cross. He knows that Peter will deny him three times. One of his close friends, Judas, will betray him. Nothing surprises Jesus.

The second theme is the weakness of the disciples. The disciples can't stay awake to pray with Jesus. Though Jesus has told them clearly, the disciples have no idea he is about to be arrested and crucified. Judas, who is greedy, has no idea he is betraying the Son of God. After Jesus's arrest, the disciples scatter. Weak and afraid, Peter denies knowing Jesus three times. The disciples need the Holy Spirit's power for courage, guidance and understanding.

Finally, we see the fulfillment of God's plan. Jesus is betrayed by Judas, and Peter denies ever knowing him. After the resurrection, Jesus teaches the disciples who walk the road to Emmaus, how all the Scriptures (Old Testament) point to his coming and mission. It is not until after Jesus rises from the dead and he appears to them, that the disciples begin to understand his true mission.

The Trap

If a squirrel finds its way into your attic, other squirrels might soon follow. Before long, you could have an entire attic filled with squirrels! To prevent this from happening, you need to catch the squirrel in a live trap and relocate it to where it belongs.

The scribes and elders treated Jesus like a squirrel in an attic. They didn't want him teaching in the temple. They were afraid his teaching would spread to all the people, and they would start following Jesus instead of them. They didn't like that Jesus came in and overturned the tables of the money changers. They wondered, Who did Jesus think he was, behaving that way in the temple? They wanted to get rid of him, and fast. So they tried to trap Jesus with a question, in hopes that they could arrest him. "Who gave you the authority to do these things?" they asked.

They thought they could trap Jesus, but Jesus was too smart for them. He fired back with a question of his own—one he knew they could not answer. When they refused to answer, Jesus also refused to answer their question. The religious rulers discovered that it's impossible to fool Jesus, and you certainly can't trap God. This is a lesson we should remember, too. God knows and sees all things—even our hearts.

A Picture of Jesus

When you look into a mirror, you see a reflection of yourself. The image looks just like you! Some stories are like mirrors. They reflect a picture of a deeper truth. Jesus told the temple rulers a story like that. At first it seemed like a story about a farmer, but it actually reflected the life of Jesus. It also reflected the very rulers who were trying to kill him. Do you see them pictured in the story?

The man in the parable who planted the vineyard represented God. The lending of the vineyard to the tenant represented a blessing to Israel. The three servants who he sent back for a portion of the harvest were a picture of the prophets God sent to Israel. Notice how patient the owner was with the wicked tenants. Finally, he sent his son, who was a picture of Jesus.

When the son arrived, the tenants killed him. In telling this parable, Jesus was predicting his own death. Jesus also used the parable to warn the temple rulers. By the time he finished, they realized he was talking about them. They were the wicked tenants reflected in the story. Since they have rejected Jesus, the owner (God) will destroy them and give the blessing of the vineyard to others (the Gentiles). When you hear stories about Jesus from the Bible, how do you respond? Do you welcome him, or reject him?

God Knows the Future

People love to try and predict who will win a game. Sometimes a game comes down to one play. In a tied soccer game, if a player can score a last-minute goal, their team will win. If they fail, the game could end in a tie. We watch the last minute because we don't know what will happen. The best we can do is hope or guess. God, on the other hand, knows all things; he knows the end from the beginning. He knows who will win every game, for he knows the future.

In our Scripture today, Jesus foretold that the city of Jerusalem would be conquered and the temple destroyed. He also added a warning that one day God will judge the whole earth. Everyone will stand before Jesus, the Son of Man, to be judged (Luke 21:36). Jesus wasn't guessing what will happen; he knows the future. He told his disciples, "Heaven and earth will pass away, but my words will not pass away" (v. 33). Today, we are still waiting for Jesus's return, reading the words he spoke from Luke's gospel. Jesus was right; his word has not passed away. We have it written down in our Bibles!

Forty years after he predicted the destruction of the temple, the temple was set on fire and it and the city of Jerusalem were destroyed. The historian Josephus saw it with his own eyes. He wrote "Caesar gave orders that they should now demolish the entire city and Temple." He said the Romans tore down the walls all the way to the ground so that a visitor to Jerusalem would not know that anyone had lived there. One day, just as Jesus said, he will return to judge the earth. Are you ready?

The Betrayal

Try to hold thirty nickels in one hand. They are about the same size as the thirty silver denarius coins the chief priests offered Judas to betray Jesus (Matthew 26:15). It is sad to think Judas betrayed Jesus for a handful of coins. Sin blinds us and leads us astray.

Judas wasn't the only one to sin in our Bible passage. The disciples argued about who was the greatest (Luke 22:24). Peter boasted that he would follow Jesus to prison and even death, but Jesus knew he would deny him before the rooster crowed (v. 34). Our Bible story shows that we are all sinners who need forgiveness. We too are like the disciples. Sin leads us astray. We disobey God's commands, get angry, and boast. Jesus wasn't surprised that the disciples were sinners. That is why he came to die—to take the punishment we deserve.

When Jesus shared the bread, he said, "This is my body which is given for you" (Luke 22:19). The bread represents Jesus's body broken on the cross to take our punishment. He took the cup and said, "This cup that is poured out for you is the new covenant in my blood" (v. 20). A covenant is a promise. God promises that all who trust in the death of Jesus for the forgiveness of their sin will be saved (Acts 16:31). Like the disciples, we are all sinners. Will we, like Peter, turn from our sin to trust Jesus, or will we turn away from Jesus like Judas? Only those who turn from their sin and believe will be saved.

CAPTAIN'S NOTE

Jesus also said, "Do this in remembrance of me'" (Luke 22:19). We obey this command during our Sunday gathering when we celebrate the Lord's Supper (some call it Communion).

Peter's Fall

Imagine your mom is preparing to bake a cake but is called away to take a phone call. You see the eggs set out on the counter. You start playing with the eggs when one slips out of your hand, rolls across the counter, and falls to the floor and breaks. You quickly slip out of the room, hoping it will look like the egg rolled off the counter on its own. You are afraid. You don't want to confess the truth, and you especially don't want to get into trouble.

Peter denied Jesus because he was afraid that telling the truth would get him into trouble. Jesus was arrested as a criminal. If Peter said he was with Jesus, the soldiers could arrest him too. Earlier, Peter boasted that he would go to prison or even die for Jesus (Luke 22:33). Peter thought Jesus would fight back. When Jesus didn't call down angels from heaven, and told the disciples to put away their swords, Peter became afraid. That is why he lied. But when the rooster crowed, he realized his big mistake.

Jesus didn't fight back. Instead, he chose to take the punishment we deserved. He came to save us. Jesus fulfilled the words of Isaiah, "like a lamb that is led to the slaughter, and like a sheep that before its shearers is silent, so he opened not his mouth" (Isaiah 53:7).

CAPTAIN'S NOTE

Read Isaiah 53 and Psalm 22 with the cross in mind. It is amazing to me that Isaiah wrote more than 700 years before Jesus, and David wrote his Psalm 1,000 years before Jesus. Long before Jesus was born, these men foretold of the crucifixion in great detail. That's because God planned to save us through the cross.

The Trial of Jesus

A witness is a person who saw or heard something. A person who witnesses a bank robbery might be asked to share their story in court—to identify the person they saw run out of the bank with the money. A false witness is someone who does not tell the truth to the judge. The people called to speak at Jesus's trial were false witnesses, for they did not tell the truth.

Matthew tells us, "Now the chief priests and the whole council were seeking false testimony against Jesus that they might put him to death, but they found none, though many false witnesses came forward" (Matthew 26:59–60).

Pilate was not fooled by the false witnesses. He could tell Jesus didn't do anything wrong. In fact, he wanted to let Jesus go. But the crowd, stirred up by the religious rulers, shouted, "Crucify him!" (Luke 23:21). Finally, Pilate gave in to the demands of the crowd and sent Jesus to be nailed to a cross and left to die, even though he was innocent (Luke 22:24).

The Choice

Life is full of choices. We choose what to wear each day. We choose what to eat for breakfast. And we choose each word we speak. But there is one choice more important than all the rest. Will we choose to believe and trust in Jesus, or reject him and go our own way? The Bible tells us we must choose between the way of life and the path that leads to death (Matthew 7:13–14).

The two thieves crucified with Jesus had one day left to choose. Would they turn from their sin and put their trust in Jesus, or reject him? We know of course that only one of the robbers chose to turn from his sin and believe. The second criminal mocked Jesus and chose the path of death, for those who turn away from Jesus will not be saved.

Each of us has this same most-important choice to make. We can choose the path of life, which is a path of blessing, and put our trust in Jesus; or we can choose the path of death, which is a path of darkness. Once you know the truth, there is no good reason to walk down the dark path. Let us make the same choice as the repentant man on the cross. Let us choose Jesus and the path of life. Here are a few questions to ponder: What is the benefit of choosing Jesus now? What is the benefit of walking with him all our days? Why is this choice more important than all others?

Prove It to Me

Anyone can claim to be able to shoot three arrows and land all three in the center of the bull's-eye. If someone made that claim, you might not believe them. But if you witness the same person shoot three arrows into the very center of a target, then they prove that their words are true.

Jesus's resurrection is the proof that all he said and did was true. Jesus told his disciples, "The Son of Man must suffer many things and be rejected by the elders, the chief priests and the teachers of the law, and he must be killed and on the third day be raised to life" (Luke 9:22 NIV). Jesus proved his words when he rose from the grave. The angels that greeted the women at the empty tomb reminded them, "Remember how he told you, while he was still in Galilee, that the Son of Man must be delivered into the hands of sinful men and be crucified and on the third day rise" (Luke 24:6–7).

The soldiers guarding Jesus's tomb witnessed the power of his resurrection (Matthew 28:4). Mary Magdalene spoke with the risen Jesus at the tomb (John 20:15). The disciples saw Jesus after he rose, and ate with him (John 21:12). Jesus even appeared to more than 500 people at the same time (1 Corinthians 15:6). It is easy to say you will rise from the dead, but Jesus proved his claim by actually doing it. Now he calls all of us to believe as well!

The Road to Emmaus

Pin the Tail on the Donkey is a popular children's party game. One by one, children are given a tail they need to pin on the back of the donkey picture. But first, they are blindfolded and spun around a couple of times to confuse them. It is fun to watch children put the tail on the donkey's ears, nose, and just about everywhere but where it belongs.

The disciples in our story were confused and blinded from the truth. Even though Jesus taught that his death was a part of God's plan, the disciples didn't understand until after he rose. In today's story, the Bible says that as they walked beside Jesus, their eyes "were kept from recognizing him" (Luke 24:16). Jesus told them that it was their unbelief that hindered them (v. 25). Their walk on that road is a picture of our lives. We are all blinded by the sin of unbelief (lack of faith). We need the Holy Spirit to open our eyes and hearts to the truth of the gospel. Jesus later told Paul that he was sending him to "open the eyes" of those who do not believe, "so that they may turn from darkness to light and from the power of Satan to God" (Acts 26:18a).

The Holy Spirit working through the gospel story of Jesus, has the power to lift the blindfold of unbelief from our eyes. Jesus explained to the disciples how the whole Bible points to him. The truth of the gospel touched their hearts. When Jesus broke bread, they recognized him, for the Holy Spirit opened their eyes to see and believe.

CAPTAIN'S NOTE

Read Mark 9:30-32 to see where Jesus predicted his death.

Jesus Is the Real Deal

One of the ways to test whether a gold bar is real, is to weigh it. Gold is heavy and you can feel its weight in your hand. Another way to prove gold is genuine, is to drill a hole and inspect the shavings that come from inside. If the pieces that come from the center are grey like lead, and not yellow, you know the bar is a fake, only covered with a thin plating of gold. But if the shavings are bright yellow, you know the bar is real.

When Jesus appeared to the disciples after he rose from the dead, they did not believe it was him. They thought he was a ghost (Luke 24:37). To prove he was real, Jesus held out

his hands and showed them his feet and said, "touch me, and see" (v. 39). The disciples were amazed but still did not believe. So, to help prove to them he was real, Jesus asked them for something to eat, and he ate a piece of fish for all to see.

But more than him showing his hands or eating the fish, Jesus opened the Scriptures to explain the gospel. Just as he did with the disciples on the road to Emmaus, Jesus explained how the Bible was about him, his death, and resurrection. He opened their minds (v. 45) to understand the gospel—that those who turn from their sin and trust in Jesus will be forgiven.

CAPTAIN'S NOTE *The whole Old Testament points forward to Jesus. Read the following Old Testament Bible verses to see how they point to Jesus: Isaiah 7:14 and 61:6; and Psalm 16:10 and 22:16-18.*

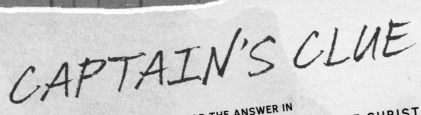

CAPTAIN'S CLUE

SEARCH FOR THE ANSWER IN

LUKE PART FIVE: THE DEATH AND VICTORY OF CHRIST

CLUE:

Jesus taught of his death
as part of God's plan.
But not until this time
did they understand.

They did not understand until __ __ter he rose from the dead.

__ __ter is the next part of the riddle.

Now let's put it together with what you have so far.

discover my treasure written
in stone __ __ter

Another Journal

After a busy morning weeding and tending to the farm, Theos and Mira sat down with Lydia to read the next entry in the Captain's journal.

Lydia opened to the bookmarked page from the day before. As Theos waited for her to begin, he slipped his hand into his pocket. He felt for the doubloon from Andros. He was excited to work on the next clue.

"There is a note from the Captain," Lydia said looking down where they left off.

She read aloud: *I hope you enjoyed the gospel of Luke. Now move on to my second journal to continue your search for the treasure.*

"Second journal?! What second journal?!" Theos shouted.

"I'm not sure," Lydia answered.

"May I see it?" Theos asked. Lydia handed him the book. Theos paged through the rest of the journal. There were no more clues. When he flipped to the last page, he looked distressed. "What second book?" he asked again.

Mira answered, "Maybe we missed it."

"Missed what?" Theos said, growing impatient.

"Can I see?" Mira asked as she held out her hand for the journal. Theos passed the leather-bound book to his sister.

Mira quickly flipped back to the beginning and read from the Captain's introduction. "Along with the scrolls, I leave you my journals." Mira pointed to the word journals. "It's plural. There is an 's' on the end of the word journal. There must be two journals, one for the book of Luke and a second for the book of Acts. We only have the first."

"We must go find it!" Theos shouted. "Before Andros starts distributing the doubloons and people start poking around!" He pulled the coin out of his pocket to make his point.

"Can we go, Mom?" Mira asked.

"I'm afraid not," Lydia answered. She pointed to the clock. "The tide is rolling in and the waves will be crashing against the rocks. It's not safe. Low tide will not return until after dark. We'll need to wait until tomorrow when the tide runs low in daylight."

"But the waves could wash away the journal," Theos pleaded.

"If you are meant to find that second book, it will be there," Lydia said as she ran her hand along Theos's shoulder.

"It will be soaked for sure," Mira said.

"We can spread out the pages and dry it," Theos reasoned with a hopeful tone. He stood up and moved to a window and looked toward the sea. If only he had looked through to the bottom of the jar.

Mira walked to the window and put her arm around Theos. "It will be there," she said. "We were meant to find that jar." Then she added, "There is no luck, no accident,

nor random chance. Every detail of life is woven by God's hand." The motto Mira memorized from the ship comforted Theos.

"You're right," he replied. "It'll be there."

Lydia looked at her two children standing at the window arm in arm. She questioned how they'd ever find it, but she vowed to continue their study with or without the journal. She couldn't help but think that everything seemed to be unfolding according to some mysterious plan . . .

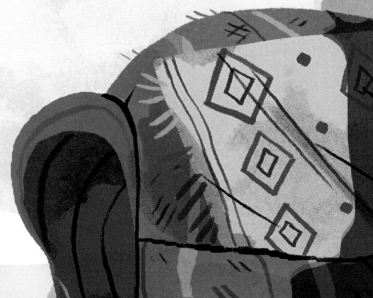

BOOK TWO

An Adventure through the Book of Acts

CHAPTER 7

Back to the Sea

Theos walked ahead of his mother and sister, eager to reach the place where they first discovered the journal and scrolls. It had been weeks since they first retrieved them from the ship's water jar. Theos hoped he would find the second journal at the bottom of the vessel, under the broken pieces of clay.

"This is it!" shouted Mira against the rumble of waves in the distance. "This is where I found the rocks that broke the jar. We're close!"

"Let's hurry," said Lydia, scrambling over the grassy bluff, down the rocky hill to the sea.

Theos joined his mom, with Mira close behind. "I'll show you. I know just where it is," he said. Theos leapt from one rock to another.

"Careful," said Lydia. "The rocks are slippery."

"I know, Mom," he answered as he zipped along the boulders and dropped down onto a narrow path that ran like a maze through the gaps.

"I can see it!" he shouted, with Mira scrambling close behind.

The jar sat right where they left it, covered in sand. Shards of broken pottery poked out of the sand like shark's teeth. Theos moved a large piece, exposing a hole. He thrust his hand right into the jar.

"Ouch!" screamed Theos, waving his hand in the air. A yellow sea snake clamped to his wrist and wriggled. Theos shook his hand again and again, but the snake would not let go.

"Get off!" Theos shouted as he battered the snake to the ground.

Suddenly, the snake vanished from sight. Theos shook his hands and feet, heart racing. He glanced to his left and right. He took a deep breath. Then he came to his senses. He opened his eyes and realized he

was at home, in his bedroom, in his bed. It had only been a dream.

Later that morning, Theos shared his dream with Mira over breakfast.

"I warned you not to put your hand in that jar," she reminded him as she finished the last bite of scrambled eggs.

Theos, Mira, and Lydia left the breakfast dishes in the sink and headed for the shoreline. It was as though Theos retraced the steps of his dream. Only this time, he would look before reaching into the jar.

After scrambling down the stones, the three made their way to the location where the children had first discovered the large clay jar.

"There it is!" Mira shouted. "I can see the top of it, but the rest is covered."

"It's filled with sand," Theos shouted as he pushed ahead and plopped down, wiping away the sand.

"Careful, Theo," Mira reminded him. "No snakes. Ok?"

Theos stopped his digging and looked around at the edges of the rocks. "No snakes," he said. He spied a pointed fragment of the jar. He picked it up and began to use it to scoop out the sand from inside the vessel.

Lydia offered a prayer, "Oh, please let us find it."

Scoop after scoop of sand flew about as Theos worked like a machine.

Lydia's heart sank when she heard Theos scrape the bottom.

"It's not here," Theos said defeated. "It's empty." A tear ran down his face.

"Are you sure?" Mira asked and thrust her hand into the jar. She ran her fingers all around the bottom, but found nothing. "It's gone," she agreed.

Theos rose and brushed the sand from his palms. "We'll just have to find the treasure with the first half of the riddle: *Discover my treasure, written in stone, after.*"

"Maybe there is something carved into one of these old rocks," Lydia suggested.

The three began searching the boulders for a hidden message or clue.

"Keep your eyes out for the journal; it could be anywhere wedged among these rocks," Theos said as he searched. He wasn't about to give up.

"Looking for this?" a booming voice called down, scaring the three half to death. A loud bark sounded from just over the bluff. It was Pastor Thomas and Salty!

"I figured you might come looking for the second journal once you finished the first," Pastor Thomas said. "Salty heard you coming and let me know you were here."

Theos scurried up the rocks and threw his arms around Salty, who was wagging his tail. Salty licked Theos's face. Pastor Thomas continued, "I was watching the day you discovered the jar. You left the second journal right here without ever realizing it."

Theos couldn't believe it!

"Here you go," said Pastor Thomas, handing the journal to Theos.

"Now we'll surely find the treasure!" Theos shouted while turning to the journal's first page. "It starts with a note from the Captain, just like the first one!" Then he read the inscription aloud:

It's time to continue your quest. Read each page carefully, for by answering all the questions, you will soon solve the riddle. And once the riddle is solved, you will know the location of the hidden treasure.

All the best!
Captain Theophilus

"Well, you guys should really get moving," said Pastor Thomas. "You must be eager to solve the next clue."

"Wait!" said Theos. "How did you know there was a second journal?"

Pastor Thomas replied, "Look, I know you have a ton of questions. I'll stop by soon for a visit. I promise. But for now, I'm late for an appointment. Come, Salty! Pastor Jones is probably up at the church waiting for us."

With that, Pastor Thomas turned back up the hill. Theos, Mira, and Lydia stood speechless, stunned by the turn of events.

"Better start for home," Lydia suggested. "We've got a treasure to find."

"Yes!" Theos shouted.

"Woo-hoo!" shouted Mira.

Then the three returned home, eager to discover the next clue in the search for the Treasure of Theophilus.

• PART ONE •

The Church Is Born

Luke begins the book of Acts as he did his gospel, with another greeting to Theophilus. This shows us that Acts is meant to be part two of Luke. Even though these two books are split by John's gospel, together, they form one story. Think of Acts as the second act of a play.

Acts picks up where the gospel of Luke ended, with the ascension of Jesus into heaven. The command to share the message of Jesus, and to wait for the Holy Spirit (Luke 24:46–49) are repeated in Acts 1:5–8. The main theme of Acts is found in verse 8: The Holy Spirit empowered the disciples to proclaim the gospel to the nations.

The Ascension

READ Luke 24:50–53 and Acts 1:6–11

Helium is lighter than air. Just as an air bubble rises in a fish tank, a helium balloon will rise into the sky if you let go of its string. But if you tie the string to the end of a spool of fishing line, you can let the balloon go and watch it rise to the clouds. With the spool, you can pull it back again. As you reel in the string, the balloon will return with it.

When Jesus left the earth to return to heaven, he rose into the clouds, just like a helium balloon floats to the sky. The disciples were

shocked to see Jesus rise and disappear. Suddenly, two angels appeared and reminded the disciples of something Jesus had taught them. They said, "This Jesus, who was taken up from you into heaven, will come in the same way as you saw him go into heaven" (Acts 1:11b). The disciples remembered that Jesus had said that the angels would sound the trumpet and all the peoples of the world would see the "Son of Man coming on the clouds of heaven with power and great glory" (Matthew 24:30b).

With Jesus gone, it was time to wait in Jerusalem for the Holy Spirit. Then the disciples would go into all the world to tell others about Jesus until the day of his return. Jesus has given us the same mission. Today we are still sharing the gospel with as many as we can until Jesus returns. No one knows when that will be; only God the Father knows the day and the hour (Mark 13:32). Until we hear the trumpet blast and see Jesus return on the clouds, we should ask the Holy Spirit to give us courage to tell everyone about Jesus.

A New Apostle

Nine players take the field in a baseball game. If one of them is injured and leaves the game, the manager will replace them. You can't play well with eight players. So, the manager chooses a player off the bench to take their place. The players on the bench have practiced with the team and traveled with them for the whole season, so they are ready to step in and play.

Just like a baseball manager, Peter told the other ten apostles that they needed to find a replacement for Judas. (Judas was the one who had turned away from Jesus and betrayed him.) The replacement, Peter said, must have two qualities. First, he must have been with them from the beginning. But most important, he must be a witness to the resurrection of Jesus. That meant he must have seen Jesus after he rose from the dead. That way, he could join the other apostles in sharing about Jesus's resurrection.

Two men were put forward: Joseph and Matthias. Unsure which one to choose, the disciples cast lots. One way to cast lots is by using sticks. To choose between two people, collect two sticks, one shorter than the other. Keeping the stick ends hidden in your hand, so they look the same length, have each person choose one of the sticks. The person who picks the shorter stick is chosen. Since God is in control of all things, the one chosen by lot would be the Lord's choice (Acts 1:24). Matthias was chosen; he replaced Judas to complete the team of twelve apostles.

CAPTAIN'S NOTE

Remember what the plaque said on The Providence? "There is no luck, no accident, nor random chance, but every detail of life is woven by God's hand into the tapestry of his plan." This is an example of how God is in control of all things.

The Holy Spirit Comes

When the Holy Spirit arrived at Pentecost, Luke writes that "tongues as of fire appeared" and "rested on each one of them" (Acts 2:3b). That sounds like what happens when fresh logs are placed onto a fire in a fireplace. The heat from the coals forces gas out of the wood. When the gas catches fire, wisps of flame, like tongues of fire, dance above the logs.

Jesus promised that God the Father would send his Holy Spirit (John 14:26). Before that, Old Testament prophets foretold of the Spirit's coming through the words of God: "I will pour my Spirit upon your offspring, and my blessing on your descendants" (Isaiah 44:3b). And, "I will put my Spirit within you, and cause you to walk in my statutes and be careful to obey my rules" (Ezekiel 36:27). When Peter stood before the crowd to explain what was happening, he reminded them of the words God had spoken through the prophet Joel: "In the last days . . . I will pour out my Spirit on all people. Your sons and daughters will prophesy, your young men will see visions, your old men will dream dreams" (Acts 2:16–17 NIV).

Today, the Holy Spirit comes to live in everyone who turns from their sin and believes in Jesus (Luke 2:38). The Jews who received the Holy Spirit at Pentecost were direct descendants of the prophets, but we also share in the same promise. We are the ones Peter described as "all who are far off" (Luke 2:39).

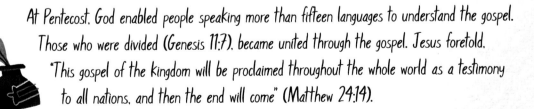

CAPTAIN'S NOTE

At Pentecost, God enabled people speaking more than fifteen languages to understand the gospel. Those who were divided (Genesis 11:7), became united through the gospel. Jesus foretold, "This gospel of the kingdom will be proclaimed throughout the whole world as a testimony to all nations, and then the end will come" (Matthew 24:14).

Peter Preaches the Gospel

The monarch caterpillar is rather ugly. It has yellow black and white stripes and two long skinny horns pointing out of its head and tail. All it does all day is eat and eat and eat. But once fully grown, it drops its skin and goes to sleep in a see-through case the size of a thimble. Then, in a week or two, it changes from a pocket of light green slime to a beautiful orange monarch butterfly. The change is amazing!

Peter went through his own amazing change after the Holy Spirit filled him. Do you remember Peter warming himself by the fire at Jesus's trial? He denied knowing Jesus three times. But after the Holy Spirit filled Peter, he stood before the crowd at Pentecost and preached about Jesus with great boldness. First, Peter told the crowd the bad news—that they were sinners. They were the ones who killed Jesus (Acts 2:23). Then Peter told them the good

news, that Jesus didn't stay dead in the grave. He was alive, and Peter and the other disciples had seen him with their own eyes!

When the people heard this gospel message, they were "cut to the heart," and asked Peter, "what shall we do?" (Acts 2:37). Peter gave them the same instructions then that we still need today. He said, "Repent [turn away from sin] and be baptized every one of you in the name of Jesus Christ for the forgiveness of your sins, and you will receive the gift of the Holy Spirit. For the promise is for you and for your children and for all who are far off, everyone whom the Lord our God calls to himself" (vv. 38–39).

CAPTAIN'S NOTE

Notice how the Holy Spirit changed Peter. He went from denying Jesus to boldly preaching about him. When we believe, God places his Spirit in our hearts, too! The Spirit changes us much like he did Peter.

The Church Begins

If you plant a small mint shoot in your garden, it will send out roots in all directions. In a few short months, it will triple in size and multiply to fill the air with a minty scent. You can dig out the side shoots and give them to your friends who can start their own mint gardens.

The early church was a lot like the mint plant. When Peter shared the gospel at Pentecost, three thousand people believed and were baptized. They became the first church plant. Just as mint multiplies and grows, the members of this first church multiplied and grew. Just like a mint plant spreads its aroma throughout the garden, the early church spread the love of Jesus throughout the community. People watching saw the new church members sharing meals, praying, and enjoying fellowship with glad hearts. This made them want to join, as well.

As the people of the early church shared the gospel message of Jesus's death and resurrection, Luke tells us that the Lord "added to their number day by day those who were being saved" (Acts 2:47b). In this way, the church grew and grew, spreading the fragrance of God's love—just as mint plants fill the air with the aroma of mint.

Peter and John Went to Pray

At a surprise birthday party, the guest of honor thinks they are going for a normal visit with a friend or family member. But when they walk through the front door, all their friends and family jump up and shout, "Surprise!" It is fun to watch the look of shock on their face.

Imagine the look of surprise on the face of the lame man from our Bible story when Peter pulled him up from where he was sitting. The lame man had asked for money, but Peter and John gave him something greater; they healed his crippled legs. The man was so excited to be healed that he began jumping and praising God. The noise got everyone's attention. They recognized the lame man and were amazed that he was walking.

Peter was quick to glorify God and share the good news of the gospel with the people at the temple. He reminded them of Jesus's death on the cross, but then told the crowd that God had raised Jesus from the dead. He said, "It is Jesus' name and the faith that comes through him that has completely healed him, as you can all see" (Acts 3:16b NIV). Then Peter challenged the crowd to turn from their wicked ways and believe in Jesus, so that their sins would be forgiven (v. 19).

Jesus Is the Only Way

Some small islands have only one bridge connecting them to the mainland. If you ask someone for directions to the island, they will tell you the bridge is the only way. When it comes to getting to heaven, Jesus is also the only way. That is what Peter told the religious rulers after his arrest.

After the lame man was healed, the priests and temple guards went to see what all the fuss was about. They heard Peter teaching that Jesus rose from the dead, and they didn't like it. So, they arrested Peter and John. The next day, the priests asked them, "By what power or by what name did you do this?" (Acts 4:7b). Peter answered, "By the name of Jesus" (v. 10). Then he told the priests, "There is salvation in no one else, for there is no other name under heaven given among men by which we must be saved" (v. 12).

The religious rulers thought they had another way to get to heaven. They thought their good works would save them. If they followed the law, God would see their good deeds and welcome them into heaven. But no one can follow the law perfectly; we are all sinners who break God's law. Peter was clear: The only way to get to heaven is by trusting in Jesus's perfect record—that he died on the cross to take the penalty for our sin. This ensures our forgiveness and welcome into heaven.

CAPTAIN'S NOTE

Jesus said, "No one comes to the Father except through me" (John 14:6b).

Sharing

Sharing is a loving thing to do, but it is rarely easy. Since we are all born as sinners with selfish hearts, we want to keep all that we have for ourselves. If we have two toys, we usually want to keep both. But when we turn from our sin and trust in Jesus, he gives us strength and compassion to share with others.

That is what happened to the new believers of the early church. They were selling extra land and sharing with those in need. Luke tells us they were "all filled with the Holy Spirit" (Acts 4:31) and "great grace was upon them all" (v. 33). Whenever our selfish hearts refuse to share, we need to remember Jesus. He gave up his life for us (John 3:16). The grace to share comes from looking back at God's generosity in giving up his Son Jesus.

The Holy Spirit reminds us that God gave his only Son, Jesus to die on the cross for us (Titus 2:14). When our eyes are open to see how generous God was in giving his Son, it makes us want to follow his example. We share with others because God first shared with us. He loved us so much that he shared his only Son. Through believing in him, our record of sin is wiped clean. God's amazing gift inspires us to share with others.

Purify the Church (Ananias and Sapphira)

Leaky, drippy pipes can ruin an entire house. As the water soaks elements of the house, mold can grow. Mold sends spores into the air and people can become sick. The only way to stop mold from spreading is to remove the broken pipe, replace it with a new one, and clean out the mold.

Sin spreads like mold; it ruins everything it touches. That is why God deals with Ananias and Sapphira so severely. Remember how the people of the new church were sharing all they had with each other? The selfishness and lies of Ananias and Sapphira had the potential to spread and tempt others to sin, too. This could have destroyed the young church.

Ananias and Sapphira didn't have to share all the money from the land they sold. It would have been fine for them to tell Peter they had sold their land and were giving *half* the money to the poor. But they wanted to look good, so they lied, and while keeping some of the money for themselves, they announced they had given all the money away. They forgot that God is holy and will not allow sin to spread in his church like mold on a damp wall. They forgot that God knows all things. You can't hide your sin from God. God is gracious and slow to anger, but he won't allow his church to be destroyed by evil.

CAPTAIN'S NOTE

Jesus told Peter that he would not allow the church to be defeated: "And I tell you, you are Peter, and on this rock I will build my church, and the gates of hell shall not prevail against it" (Matthew 16:18).

You Can't Stop the Church

The level of the ocean rises and falls at the shoreline two times every day. In some places, the ocean rises and falls only a little. But in Canada's Bay of Fundy, the ocean rises and falls over fifty feet! Each high tide, billions of tons of water rage back into the bay, and no one can stop it. More water flows during high tide than the flow of all the rivers in the world combined! The sea is that powerful.

The church is a powerful force like the ocean. Some might try to stop it, but they can't. The high priest and the other religious rulers tried to stop the spread of the new church. After Peter proclaimed the gospel at the temple, the church grew from 3,000 to 5,000 people in a short time (Acts 4:4). The religious rulers became jealous and arrested the apostles (Acts 5:17–18). They thought they could stop the spread of the gospel by putting the apostles in jail, but they learned the church is like the tide; it can't be stopped. God sent an angel to release them. Once the apostles were freed, the angel didn't tell them to run and hide; he told the apostles to return to the temple to continue sharing about Jesus.

When the religious rulers found the apostles preaching again, they questioned them. They planned to kill them, but a wise teacher named Gamaliel sent a warning, telling them to leave the apostles alone. If their mission is from God, he reasoned, they would not be able to stop them. In fact, he warned, "You might even be found opposing God!" (v. 39). Gamaliel recognized the tide of the gospel.

Caring for the Widows

Bicycles require care and maintenance. When a tire goes flat, it must be pumped with air. If the chain pops off, you must fix it before riding. The growing church in today's story also needed care and maintenance. When a conflict arose about food for the widows, the apostles came up with a solution.

They told the people to choose seven men to serve the widows, to ensure they were all treated fairly. The apostles said that those chosen should possess three qualities. First, they must be of "good repute" (Acts 6:3). That means they should be faithful and respected by the people. Second, they should be filled with the Holy Spirit. The Holy Spirit helps God's people see their sin, reminds them of Jesus's words, and teaches how to apply his truth to daily life. Third, they should be full of wisdom, which flows from applying God's Word to life.

In our own lives, conflicts arise when things don't go our way. But with God's Word and the help of the Holy Spirit, we too can grow in wisdom. As we live for Jesus, the people around us will see the grace of God in our lives, and we will become people of good repute, respected by others.

CAPTAIN'S CLUE

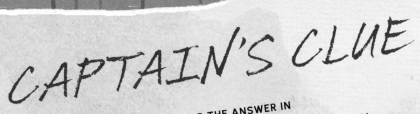

SEARCH FOR THE ANSWER IN

ACTS PART ONE: THE CHURCH IS BORN

CLUE:

Upon this thing Jesus built
the church of God, he taught.
No evil would come against
the ones his blood had bought.

Jesus said, "and on this R __ __ k I will build my church."

the R __ __ k is the next part of the riddle.

Now let's put it together with what you have so far.

discover my treasure written
in stone after the R __ __ k

The Surprise

Storms had kept Theos and Mira cooped up inside for weeks. Now, they sat on the sofa as Lydia finished reading Acts chapter nine from the scroll—the story of Jesus appearing to Saul on the road to Damascus. Then she picked up the journal and read the following captain's note:

Having read the story of Paul's conversion, I see that God is able to save even the vilest of men. If Jesus can save Saul, he can save me, too. Looking back, I clearly see the hand of God's providence at work in my life. For it was God's plan that I took Cristobal and his family upon my ship. God knew Cristobal would read from the scrolls, and he knew they would soften my hardened heart. What the Bible says sure is true: God makes everything happen just as he decided long ago. .

So now, Theos, Mira, and Lydia: Do you see God's providence at work in your life as well?

Lydia stood up suddenly and froze. Her face turned pale and she lost her grip on the journal, which dropped to the floor. Theos quickly retrieved it and reread the page.

"My name is here. All of our names are here!" Theos exclaimed. "How can that be?"

"Providence," answered Mira.

Regaining her composure, Lydia reached for the book. "May I?" she asked. Theos handed her the book. She read aloud: *"So now, Theos, Mira, and Lydia: Do you see God's providence at work in your life as well? Everything works in accordance with God's plan. He sees all, knows all, and can work every detail together for your good."*

"This is not by accident," she continued. "But how?"

"It's providence, Mom," Mira repeated. Then she quoted a portion of the ship's plaque: 'There is no luck, no accident, nor random chance. Every detail of life is woven by God's hand into the tapestry of his plan.'"

"I think Pastor Thomas knows more than he is telling us," Lydia announced. "We must visit him soon. He's got some explaining to do."

"It's low tide now. May we go out and do some more exploring?" asked Theos.

"Yes, but not too far. When I call for supper, come right home."

"Ok," Theos answered. "C'mon!" he shouted to Mira, and the two ran outside.

Theos slapped his front right pocket and felt the outline of the coin inside. Finally, now that the storms had passed, they could continue their search for the Captain's treasure.

· PART TWO ·

The Persecution and the Plan

Just before returning to heaven, Jesus told the disciples that they would be his witnesses in Jerusalem, Judea, Samaria, and to the ends of the earth (Acts 1:8). But after the Holy Spirit arrived, the disciples didn't leave as Jesus instructed. They remained in Jerusalem, teaching.

As more and more people came to believe, the religious rulers and many of the Jews did not like what the Christians were teaching. Things blew up one day when the Jews confronted Stephen, one of the disciples. They seized him and brought him before the Jewish council. Stephen defended himself and accused the religious rulers of murdering Jesus (Acts 7:52). The rulers flew into a rage and stoned Stephen to death. Then a great persecution broke out against the church in Jerusalem and many Christians were arrested and killed (Acts 8:1).

The Christians in the city were forced to scatter to Judea, Samaria, and beyond. The Jews planned to destroy the church, but God used the persecution to spread the gospel to the whole world.

Stephen's Courage

In battles of old, soldiers carried a sword and shield into battle. These two items gave them courage. The sword could be used to defeat the enemy, and the shield to defend against the enemy's attack. The apostle Paul used the example of a sword and shield to describe a Christian's battle against evil. He said that our sword is the Word of God and our shield is our faith and trust in Jesus (Ephesians 6:16–18). Stephen carried both these weapons.

Stephen was one of the men chosen to care for the widows. He was filled with the Holy Spirit and wisdom (Acts 6:3). When those who were against Stephen tried to argue with him, he used the Sword of Spirit—the Word of God—against them.

He defeated every argument they could bring. But in the end, false witnesses lied about Stephen. They rallied the people and Stephen was arrested.

Do you notice any similarities between Stephen's story and Jesus's story? Jesus was falsely accused, arrested without cause, and put on trial before the religious rulers. Jesus had said his followers would be treated poorly. Jesus taught, "Remember the word that I said to you: 'A servant is not greater than his master.' If they persecuted me, they will also persecute you" (John 15:20). Still, Stephen went into battle with courage. His shield was the faith that God would be with him, and his sword was the Word of God.

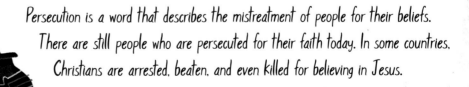

CAPTAIN'S NOTE

Persecution is a word that describes the mistreatment of people for their beliefs. There are still people who are persecuted for their faith today. In some countries, Christians are arrested, beaten, and even killed for believing in Jesus.

A History Lesson

History books record past events. A good history book tells the truth about what happened. If you read a history book about ancient Rome, it should tell the true story of how Rome became a country, and all the major events that took place until Rome was defeated. A study of history can help us learn from past mistakes and benefit from past successes. The Bible is the most famous history book of all time. It tells the true story of the people God created and his work among them. In our Bible story, Stephen used history as a defense against the Jews' accusations.

After hearing the charges against Stephen, the high priest asked, "Are these things so?" (Acts 7:1b). Stephen responded with a history lesson. He began with Abraham and shared the story of God's people, Israel. He wanted them to see that Jesus was the Messiah that God promised to send. Then, perhaps, they would welcome his message.

In his final words at his trial, Stephen rebuked the high priest by saying, "they killed those who announced beforehand the coming of the Righteous One, whom you have now betrayed and murdered, you who received the law as delivered by angels and did not keep it" (Acts 7:52b–53). Sadly, the high priest and the other religious rulers did not learn from history. Instead of welcoming Jesus as the promised Messiah, they rejected him and put him to death. Now they would do the same to Stephen.

Stephen's Death

CAPTAIN'S NOTE

As the stones began to fly, Stephen found his refuge in Jesus. This story reminds me of verse three of my favorite hymn, "Rock of Ages," which points us to find our refuge in Christ.

"While I draw this fleeting breath

When mine eyes shall close in death

When I rise to worlds unknown

And behold thee on thy throne

Rock of Ages Cleft for me

Let me hide myself in thee."

(Augustus Toplady, 1763)

Some people risk their lives doing remarkable things. Consider what mountain climbers risk as they ascend high peaks. Doctors sometimes risk their lives treating injuries in dangerous situations or tending to patients with contagious disease. Like the work of the early disciples, the call to save lives is of utmost importance.

Stephen risked his life as well. He knew he could be beaten, arrested, and even killed for telling people about Jesus. After all, Peter and John were arrested. They risked their lives sharing the gospel so that people could be rescued. They obeyed the call Jesus gave them to "go . . . and make disciples of all nations" (Matthew 28:19a). Since the day Jesus gave that command, many have given their lives for sharing their faith.

The Holy Spirit gave Stephen courage. Sadly, many of the people listening rejected the gospel, threw Stephen out of the city, and stoned him to death. Stephen gave his life so that people would hear the gospel. As the stones were hurled at him, Stephen expressed his love for and trust in Jesus. He looked to heaven and said, "'Lord Jesus, receive my spirit.' And then as he fell to his knees, he cried out with a loud voice, 'Lord, do not hold this sin against them'" (Acts 7:59–60).

The Persecution and Plan

Have you ever visited a farm in the fall with your family? Maybe you brought home some pumpkins and looked forward to roasting the seeds or making a pie. Unfortunately, before you ever get the chance, your pumpkin starts to get soft and moldy. Your parents do the only thing that makes sense; they toss the pumpkin on the backyard compost pile. However, when spring arrives, so does a surprise! A few of the pumpkin seeds have sprouted and start to grow into vines. By fall, there are a dozen pumpkins in your backyard! All your disappointment turns to joy. God turned something bad into something good.

The Bible tells us that God works all things for the good of those he loves (Romans 8:28). That is exactly what he did when Saul tried to stop the growth of the early church. When he began putting Christians in jail, the new believers scattered. They fled Jerusalem, traveling to nearby towns and villages, where they told everyone about Jesus. As a result, people in all the surrounding land learned about the Messiah. When they heard about Jesus's death and resurrection, many believed.

Sadly, Saul tried to stop the spread of the gospel by arresting Christians and putting them in jail. But the church could not be stopped. God worked Saul's evil plan for his good. Those fleeing Jerusalem spread the seeds of the gospel to the surrounding land. In the end, new churches sprouted up and grew. God turned something very bad into something very good.

CAPTAIN'S NOTE

Another story where God worked evil for good, is found in Genesis 37-45.
Joseph's brothers sold him into slavery, but God used it to save Israel from a great famine.
Joseph told his brothers, "Do not be distressed or angry with yourselves because you
sold me here, for God sent me before you to preserve life" (Genesis 45:5).

Simon the Magician

Magicians perform magic tricks. They are called tricks because they fool us. No one can really make an object float in the air and move at their command. But a magician can make an object appear to float by using a string. If the string is thin like a spider's web, the audience can't see it. The magician might appear powerful, but it is only a trick.

When Simon the magician saw the signs and miracles that Philip performed, he was amazed (Acts 8:13). Simon was famous for his magic, and many people thought his tricks were real— that Simon had the power of God (v. 10). When Simon saw the Holy Spirit come upon people at the laying on of Peter's hands, he wanted that same power for himself. So, Simon decided to offer to pay Peter and John for their power.

Peter rebuked Simon because God's power is not for sale; it is a gift. Knowing Simon was a new believer, Peter encouraged him to turn from his sin and turn to Christ. Thankfully, Simon repented and asked Peter to pray for him (Acts 8:24). Like Simon, we all make mistakes, but the Bible tells us that if we turn from our sin and confess, God is faithful to forgive us and cleanse us from all our sin (1 John 1:9).

The Ethiopian Eunuch

People hire guides to lead them on hikes through deep forests and thick jungles. The local guides know the trails and can prevent people from getting lost. Teachers are like guides who lead us through hard subjects like math, grammar, and science. In today's story, God sent Philip as a guide to an Ethiopian traveler.

The Ethiopian eunuch was reading the book of Isaiah, but he struggled to understand it. Philip led him through the Old Testament and showed how it pointed to Jesus. The lamb Isaiah spoke of (who did not fight back) was Jesus. When the soldiers came to arrest him, Jesus could have called for an army of angels to rescue him (Matthew 26:53). But instead, Jesus allowed himself to be put on trial and sent to death on a cross. Jesus took the punishment for our sins so that we could be forgiven and welcomed into the family of God.

The Ethiopian man believed this good news and became a Christian. Then, when he saw some water, he asked to be baptized. God sent Philip to guide the Ethiopian to the truth. God is still at work today helping lost sinners find their way. He uses parents, pastors, and other believers to serve as our guides, so we too can be rescued from our sin.

The Damascus Road

Our sun is a huge burning ball of fire that shines with a blinding light. It is so large, it would take 344 earths, strung like pearls, to wrap around it. The light from the sun is so bright, it can blind us. That's why adults often tell children never to look directly at the sun. The light of Jesus is even brighter than the sun!

Paul (who changed his name from Saul after becoming a Christian) shared his Damascus Road story many times. Before King Agrippa, he said, "I saw on the way a light from heaven, brighter than the sun, that shone around me and those who journeyed with me" (Acts 26:13). To the people of Jerusalem, he added: "I could not see because of the brightness of that light" (Acts 22:11a). Paul thought he could stop the spread of Christianity by arresting those who believed in Jesus. Then God blinded him with one flash of his glorious light, and his life changed forever.

One day, in the new Jerusalem, Jesus, the Lamb of God, will allow his glory to shine. John describes it like this: "The city has no need of sun or moon to shine on it, for the glory of God gives it light, and its lamp is the Lamb" (Revelation 21:23). We can't look at the sun, but in heaven we will see Jesus face to face (Revelation 22:4). We will stand in the presence of his glory around the throne and worship him (Revelation 19:6).

Changed

Every spring, the dead of winter gives way to
life and warmth. The buds on the bare branches
swell and burst forth with new green leaves. Last year's
seeds sprout with new life. The dead of winter is replaced
with new birth. A similar change happened in Saul's life.

Saul was the greatest enemy of the early church. He arrested
Christians and put them on trial. When the Christians were found guilty,
Saul approved of their deaths. But after Jesus blinded him with his glorious
light, everything changed. By the time Saul met Ananias, he was ready to
turn from his sin and believe. As Ananias prayed for Saul, God opened his
eyes to see again. Through his personal encounter with Jesus, Saul was filled
with the Holy Spirit (Acts 9:17) and brought to new life.

Saul did not waste any time. Luke tells us, "Immediately he proclaimed Jesus
in the synagogues, saying, 'He is the Son of God.' And all who heard him
were amazed and said, 'Is not this the man who made havoc in Jerusalem of
those who called upon this name?'" (Acts 9:20–21a). The wicked persecution
of Saul gave way to the life-giving preaching of Paul. Jesus would use him to
reach the Gentiles so that many would be saved (v. 15).

It's Hard to Believe

Zookeepers love to show off their animals. Consider the boa constrictor. Zookeepers drape the large snake over their shoulders and even allow children to touch it. That is something you should never do with a snake in the wild! But once you know that the snake is tame, it gives you the courage to approach it.

When Saul came to Jerusalem and wanted to meet the disciples, they were afraid. They knew he was dangerous, like a wild snake. What if he was only pretending to be safe, and would soon trap them? If they let down their guard, he might strike. But Barnabas assured them that God had indeed saved and changed Saul.

Barnabas shared how Saul now boldly proclaimed Jesus, and how some were even trying to kill him. It took some convincing, but in the end, the people believed. Jesus had tamed the great snake of a man. Convinced of this, they sent Saul on a mission to preach the gospel. With Saul on their side, the church grew in peace. The gospel spread and the church continued to multiply (Acts 9:31).

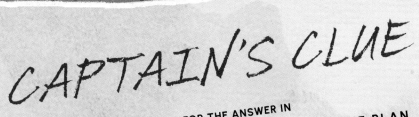

CAPTAIN'S CLUE

SEARCH FOR THE ANSWER IN

ACTS PART TWO: THE PERSECUTION AND THE PLAN

CLUE:

The next clue can be found
in my favorite hymn.
It's about a refuge
and my rock in him.

Discover your clue in the title of the hymn, Rock _ _ Ag_ _ _ is your next clue.

_ _ Ag _ _ _ is the next part of the riddle.

Now let's put it together with what you have so far.

discover my treasure written in stone
after the Rock _ _ Ag_ _ _

CHAPTER 9

The Plan

Theos and Mira scrambled over the rocks leading to the water jar.

As they climbed, Theos said, "We've got to find the treasure before a lot of people visit the museum and start searching for the Captain's gold."

When they reached the water jar, Theos retrieved the coin from his pocket and held it up against the backdrop of the island. "It's no use," he said, dropping his hands to his side.

"What's wrong?" Mira asked.

"I was afraid of this," Theos answered. "This isn't the right spot. We're too close to see the outline of the mountain."

"Let me see," Mira replied.

Theos handed his sister the plastic replica doubloon. Mira extended her hand, peering through the holes in the coin. Theos was right. She couldn't see the mountain outline.

"I can't even see over the grassy bank. Maybe we should climb further up and look from there."

"Good idea," Theos hollered while climbing up the hill. From atop the grassy bank, he could see the quarry cut into the foothills of Mt. Zeus.

"Does it match?" Mira asked.

"No. We need to be further out," Theos turned and pointed offshore.

"On that fishing boat?" Mira asked, looking at a small boat drifting just off the coast.

"Maybe that fisherman will help us. Come on, let's go back down to the shore."

Theos and Mira scrambled back down and climbed the rocks as far out as the low tide would allow. They stood on the rocks and waved their arms as they shouted to the fisherman.

"Help!" they shouted, but the fisherman did not hear them.

"Hey, Fisherman! Over here!" Mira screamed with all her might.

Mira's voice carried across the water, and the fisherman looked up from his line.

"Can you give us a ride?" Theos shouted while Mira continued jumping and waving her hands.

The fisherman smiled and waved. Then he leaned toward the rear of his boat and pulled a cord. The boat began to hum.

"He's coming!" Theos shouted as the boat turned toward shore. But his excitement gave way to disappointment as the craft circled back away and motored off.

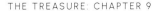

"Now what are we going to do?" Theos sighed.

"Look!" Mira shouted.

Theos lifted his gaze back to sea. Out in the distance, the island tour boat, filled with passengers, chugged along. Mira waved, and a passenger on the boat returned her greeting.

"That's it! Mira, you're a genius! We don't need the fishing boat; we need to take a ride on that boat! Let's go home and see if Mom can take us!"

When they arrived home, Theos and Mira burst through the door. Mira rattled on about the fisherman. Theos babbled endlessly about the boat tour.

Lydia couldn't understand a word they were speaking. "Slow down," she said. "One at a time."

After Mira shared the events of the afternoon, Theos asked if they could go on the first tour in the morning. Lydia agreed to take them, but only after the weekend, when the tours were less expensive.

"But we've got to get on the tour boat before too many people get their hands on these coins!" Theos displayed the doubloon from his pocket.

Lydia smiled, "All right," she said. "We'll take the first tour Monday morning. We'll beat the crowds and be off the boat before Andros can give away another coin."

Theos and Mira agreed, but they could hardly wait.

· PART THREE ·

The Gentiles

This section of the Book of Acts tells the story of Peter's ministry and God's call upon him to preach the gospel to the Gentiles. God sends Peter to a Gentile named Cornelius. To Peter's surprise, God saves Cornelius and his entire household and pours out his Spirit upon the Gentiles in the same way he did the Jews. As a result of Peter's report of this event, the Gentiles are welcomed into the church. This is a fulfillment of the word God spoke through the prophet Joel at Pentecost, "The promise is for you and for your children and for all who are far off, everyone whom the Lord our God calls to himself" (Acts 2:39).

After Peter reported these events to the church leaders, the Holy Spirit told them to send Paul and Barnabas to the Gentiles. So, after praying and laying hands on them, the church in Antioch sent Paul on his first missionary journey, with Barnabas.

This third section of the book of Acts ends at the close of Paul and Barnabas's missionary journey, with their report to the council in Jerusalem. God first called the Jews, then the Gentiles too. Today he calls you and calls me to believe and join this great family of God.

Peter's Ministry

The wax seal on a royal letter carries the king or queen's authority, and all their words must be obeyed. We still use seals today to authorize important papers. A notary is an official who affixes a seal to a paper to prove it came from the person who wrote it. You can pay a notary to witness your signing of a letter, and then set their seal upon it to prove that it came from you.

In our Bible passage, when Peter prayed for Aeneas, he didn't say "I heal you," he said, "Jesus Christ heals you" (Acts 9:34). But Jesus wasn't there; he had gone back to heaven. Peter's faith was in Jesus. Faith in Jesus is like a seal stamped on our prayers. We come by his authority. Jesus taught his disciples and said, "I will do whatever you ask in my name, so that the Father may be glorified in the Son. You may ask me for anything in my name, and I will do it" (John 14:13–14 NIV). The disciples healed in the name of Jesus and performed powerful signs. Peter commanded the crowd at Pentecost to repent "in the name of Jesus." These were the same words he spoke to the lame man at the temple, before helping him up to walk.

When we pray today, we can ask for God to move in the name of Jesus, just as the disciples prayed. That doesn't mean we can pray in Jesus's name for anything we want. Our prayers must line up with God's will and plan (1 John 5:14). But when we pray in the name of Jesus, it is as though we set our King's seal upon our prayer. The name Jesus is the greatest name in all history! Because Jesus gave up his life on the cross, Paul tells us that God the Father "gave him the name that is above every name, that at the name of Jesus every knee should bow" (Philippians 2:9b–10a NIV).

Peter's Vision

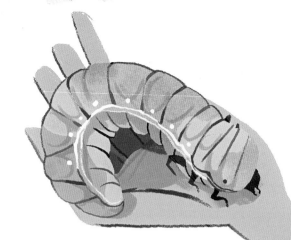

People around the world eat unusual foods. Some Malaysians eat giant sago grubs. Some people in Japan eat the eyes of fish. There are Africans who collect termites for snacks. How do these foods sound to you? If someone handed you a giant grub to eat, I'll bet you would reply, "No way! I won't eat that!" That is exactly what Peter told God in a vision when he was asked to eat unclean animals. The Old Testament Scriptures said that animals like pigs, lizards, and ravens were unclean (Leviticus 11). Peter obeyed such laws; he had no idea that God was about to change things.

God used this vision to teach Peter a lesson. God planned for the gospel to reach people from every nation, not just the Jews. In times past, God told Israel not to marry idol-worshiping people from other nations (Deuteronomy 7:3–4). Over time, the people of Israel looked down upon these Gentiles (non-Jewish people). They took God's command too far and would not even go into a Gentile's home. Since God planned to send Peter into a Gentile home to preach the gospel, Peter had to first learn that God loved the Gentiles and planned to save them too.

God told Abraham that all the nations of the earth would be blessed through him (Genesis 18:18). Jesus came from the family line of Abraham to fulfill that promise by bringing salvation to people from every nation. That is why he told the disciples to go and make disciples of all nations (Matthew 28:19a). God's vision to Peter opened his eyes to see that the gospel was meant for all people. Peter realized that "God does not show favoritism but accepts from every nation the one who fears him and does what is right" (Acts 10:34–35 NIV).

Good News

During ancient Greek wars, soldiers on horseback carried messages of good news. Parents, whose sons were in battle, waited with hope for messages of victory. When they received such news, the word *eu-an-gel-ion* was spread throughout the villages. The word *euangelion* means good news. It is the Greek word translated gospel in our Bible. Euangelion is also the Greek root for our word *evangelism*, which means sharing the good news.

In today's Scripture, Peter shared the good news with Cornelius and his family, saying, "You know the message God sent to the people of Israel, announcing the good news of peace through Jesus Christ, who is Lord of all" (Acts 10:36 NIV).

Then Peter taught how Jesus is the one God promised to send to bring an end to our battle with sin and death. Peter explained that Jesus died for our sins but then rose again in victory so that "everyone who believes in him receives forgiveness of sins through his name" (v. 43 NIV).

As Peter shared the message of the gospel (good news), the Holy Spirit filled the people and opened their eyes to believe. All at once, the people began to praise God for Jesus and his salvation. Today, the good news Peter shared with Cornelius is preserved in our Bible for us to read. Here is the good news: Jesus also died for our sins so that we can be forgiven. The big question is: *Will we believe?*

CAPTAIN'S NOTE

Isaiah prophesied about a day when the Promised One would proclaim good news. In Isaiah 40:9; 52:7; and 61:1, the prophet used the Hebrew word *basar*, which means glad tidings. When the Jews translated the Old Testament into the Greek language, they used the word *euangelion*, which means good news.

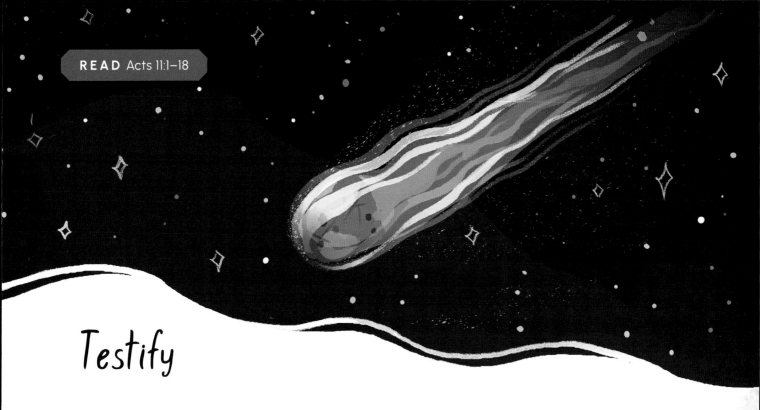

Testify

Imagine one night you see a fiery streak across the starlit sky. It's not a shooting star that quickly fades, but a comet with a flaming tail. Wouldn't you want to run inside and tell everyone? If you say, "There's a comet in the sky," people might not believe you. But if you add your eyewitness account, "I saw it with my own eyes!" your testimony is powerful. Soon other people want to see it, too!

When the apostles heard that Peter was preaching to the Gentiles, they were upset, for they believed Jews should stay away from Gentiles. But once Peter shared what he saw with his own eyes, they believed. Peter told them the whole story and how God spoke to him.

Peter finished his story by saying, "If then God gave the same gift to them as he gave to us when we believed in the Lord Jesus Christ, who was I that I could stand in God's way?" (Acts 11:17). When the apostles heard Peter's testimony of how the Holy Spirit fell upon the Gentiles, they were amazed and praised God. They believed Peter's story and rejoiced that God would save the Gentiles too.

Barnabas

Pillars are strong supports that hold up the roof of a building. Sometimes when a person serves in the church over a long period of time, they are called a "pillar in the church." This is because their service supports the church. Take the pillars out of a building, and a roof would collapse. In the same way, removing individuals serving the church, might cause the whole church to suffer.

Barnabas is a great example of a pillar in the church. When the church first began, Barnabas sold land and shared the money with the apostles (Acts 4:37). His real name was Joseph, but they called him Barnabas, which means son of encouragement (v. 36). Barnabas was the one who stood by Saul's side. He encouraged the Christians to give Saul a chance after he met Jesus on the road to Damascus.

When the leaders in Jerusalem heard that God was saving people as far away as Antioch, they sent their best, Barnabas, to care for and teach them. Once he arrived, Barnabas encouraged the new believers, and the church grew. Luke adds that Barnabas was "a good man, full of the Holy Spirit and of faith" (Acts 11:24a)— a pillar in the early church.

Peter's Escape

The lion is often called the "king of the jungle." Lions rule over the other animals and fear no one. Male lions weigh around 400 pounds, and their roar can be heard five miles away. In the book of Revelation, Jesus is called the "Lion of the tribe of Judah," a name first given by Jacob to his son Judah (Genesis 49:9).

In today's story, after King Herod murdered James, he arrested Peter. Herod thought two chains, two guards, and four squads of soldiers would be enough to guard Peter, who had escaped from prison before. But Herod was wrong. Jesus sent a single angel to break Peter out of prison (Acts 12:7). Herod thought he was the most powerful man in Jerusalem, but he was wrong. Jesus, the Lion of the tribe of Judah, ruled over Herod.

Herod thought he had plenty of life to live, but he was wrong. After breaking Peter out of prison, the Lord brought judgment upon Herod. A short time later, the Lord sent an angel to strike Herod down for not giving glory to God (Acts 12:23). We must always remember that Jesus, who rules over all as a Lion, rules over us as well. He calls all people to believe. "For we must all appear before the judgment seat of Christ, so that each one may receive what is due for what he has done in the body, whether good or evil" (2 Corinthians 5:10).

CAPTAIN'S NOTE

Lion is a fitting name for Jesus, for he rules over all (Colossians 2:10).

Jesus Our Champion

The punch of a professional boxer hits its mark with 1,000 pounds of force. That is enough power to knock a person out cold with one blow. So it is not a good idea to pick a fight with a champion boxer. In our story, Elymas, a magician, picked a fight with someone even more powerful. When Elymas opposed Barnabas and Paul and tried to stop the city governor from hearing about Jesus, he picked a fight with God.

Elymas opposed the greatest champion of all time. All it took was one stroke by the Holy Spirit to defeat him. The Spirit filled Paul, who looked at Elymas and said, "the hand of the Lord is upon you, and you will be blind and unable to see the sun for a time" (Acts 13:11a). Immediately Elymas lost his sight. When the governor saw what happened, he believed in Jesus.

The Spirit of God is still at work building the church today, calling all people to trust in Jesus. He will never lose his reputation as the greatest champion of all time—our eternal victor over sin and death.

CAPTAIN'S NOTE

Isaiah described God as a champion when he said, "The LORD goes out like a mighty man, like a man of war he stirs up his zeal; he cries out, he shouts aloud, he shows himself mighty against his foes" (Isaiah 42:13).

Antioch

The back of a piece of needlework looks very different from the front. The front displays a beautiful pattern or picture. But when you flip to the back, you see a web of interconnected strings and knots. These reveal how the artist's needle jumped from section to section and where they tied off each string. Reading a New Testament Bible story is a bit like looking at the front of needlework. But there is more to the story. Exploring how the Old Testament is connected to the New Testament, gives you a behind-the-scenes look at God's plan. That is what Paul shared with the people of Antioch.

After reading from the Old Testament, Paul told the people of Antioch that Jesus was the promised seed of King David, connecting the story of Jesus with David of the Old Testament. He explained how Psalm 2 pointed to Jesus (Acts 13:33) and how Psalm 16:2 foretold of Jesus's resurrection from the dead (v. 35).

Paul warned and challenged the crowd by quoting Habakkuk 1:5, "For I am doing a work in your days, a work that you will not believe, even if one tells it to you" (Acts 13:41b). The Gentiles rejoiced in Paul's teaching and believed (v. 48). How will you respond? Today, as you learn about God's plan of salvation, will you believe?

Paul's Hardships

CAPTAIN'S NOTE

Paul shared a list of his sufferings with the Corinthians. Read 2 Corinthians 11:24-33. Notice how Paul trusts in Christ through it all.

It is amazing to watch a craftsman carve a figure from a block of wood. At first, he removes large chunks with a bandsaw. Then, as the shape is refined, smaller and smaller chips are whittled away. Final details are cut into the piece with fine knives and files until all the waste is gone and the figure is complete. God uses the trials in our lives to refine us in similar ways. God allows hardship to shape and perfect our faith and trust in him (James 1:2–4). The Master Craftsman cuts the wood but doesn't damage the figure. That is what he did with Paul and Barnabas.

Sharing the gospel was not easy for Paul. God allowed him to endure threats, beatings, and even stoning. Through it all, God was with Paul and delivered him from many dangers. God used these terrible events for Paul's good—to strengthen his faith. Paul told the Corinthians, "He delivered us from such a deadly peril, and he will deliver us. On him we have set our hope that he will deliver us again" (2 Corinthians 1:10).

In all his hardships, Paul trusted the Lord and did not complain. He knew that one day in heaven, all his trials would come to an end. Paul taught the Corinthians, "For our light and momentary troubles are achieving for us an eternal glory that far outweighs them all" (2 Corinthians 4:17 NIV). That is why he encouraged his followers to "continue in the faith," saying that "through many tribulations we must enter the kingdom of God" (Acts 14:22b). God still uses hardship to address our unbelief and fear—to help us trust him. So, the next time we meet with troubles or difficulty, rather than complain, we should ask God for help. He can build our faith and lift our hope to heaven.

Saved by Grace

Imagine getting free tickets to
a baseball game, because of a
friend's generosity. Now you get to
go to the game for free! It wouldn't
be right for the guard at the gate to make
you pay for the tickets—the price of admission has
already been paid.

When God began saving the Gentiles, some of the Jews wanted to force them to obey the old
Jewish laws and earn their way to God. That was kind of like making them pay to get into a game,
even though they had a free ticket. Jesus died on the cross to pay for our sins. The apostle Paul
explained it this way: "For by grace you have been saved through faith. And this is not your own
doing; it is the gift of God, not a result of works, so that no one may boast" (Ephesians 2:8–9). We
don't need to keep the law perfectly; Jesus did that for us. His obedience paid for our ticket!

When the apostles and elders of the church met to discuss this, Peter, who saw God pour out his
Spirit on Cornelius, reminded them that God saved the Gentiles (Acts 15:8) without the old Jewish
ways. He said we are all saved by "the grace of the Lord Jesus" (v. 11). We are not saved by following customs or laws. The word grace means gift. So, we are saved as a "free gift" from God
(Romans 5:15). Peter's words convinced the counsel to welcome Gentiles into the church.

Send Your Best

When you go to a special event, you wear your best clothes. When you take a test in school, or you join a sports team, you should also give your best. That means working hard in practice to improve your skills, or studying hard for the test. If a mountain climber falls and is injured on a climb, the best-trained rescuers are sent to help.

In today's story, once the church council agreed to welcome the Gentiles, they sent their best leaders to train the new believers so that more people could be saved. The council chose Barnabas and Paul, two men they dearly loved (Acts 15:25). Barnabas, if you remember, was a pillar in the church, and Paul ended up writing much of our New Testament.

The council also sent two prophets, Judas and Silas, to encourage the Gentile believers (Acts 15:32). When it came to caring for the Gentile church, Peter and the other leaders sent their best. They wanted to make sure the Gentiles knew that God saved them by his free grace. No one could require them to earn or pay for their salvation through good works.

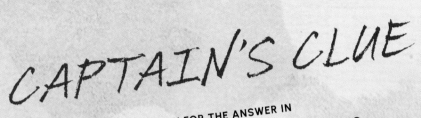

CAPTAIN'S CLUE

SEARCH FOR THE ANSWER IN

ACTS PART THREE: TO THE GENTILES

CLUE:

God called Peter to preach.
God called Paul to proclaim.
God calls you and c__l__s me
to believe in his name.

c__l__s me is the next part of the riddle.

Now let's put it together with what you have so far.

discover my treasure written in stone
after the Rock of Ages c__l__s me

The *Nerina*

During the weekend tour, the *Nerina* carried ninety passengers. But Monday's two o'clock tour left the dock with only ten: Theos, Mira, Lydia, and seven others. Theos watched them closely as they left the dock. As far as he could tell, none of them had a doubloon.

The boat followed the coast south around the point into Karades Bay. The white plastered houses glimmered against the rocky brown hills. A fine salt spray lifted into the air as the bow of the vessel cut through the sea. Once away from the dock, the captain motored for the point, pulling the throttle to full speed.

Theos slid his hand into his pocket and flipped his coin several times. He enjoyed the smell of the ocean, the call of the gulls following the *Nerina*, and the hum of the tour boat's diesel engine.

"Should we take a look?" Mira asked her brother as soon as the *Nerina* cleared the point.

"Soon," Theos answered, as Mt. Zeus came into view.

The captain turned the wheel a bit to the left and headed for the center of the bay, near where the children spotted the tour boat from on shore several days prior.

"Look!" Mira shouted. I see the church sitting on the hillside. I see Pastor Thomas's house, too!"

As the *Nerina* curved its way toward the center of the bay, Theos retrieved the doubloon from his pocket.

"This is it," he said excitedly as he held up the coin to Mt. Zeus. "The cut in the coin matches the outline!"

Mira reached for her bag. She unzipped the top and retrieved her doubloon and looked through to the outline of the mountain. "Perfect!" she said.

"Can I see?" Lydia asked Mira.

Lydia extended her arm and held the coin away from her body. "The outline does match the mountain. And the cross, too! Take a look," she said, returning the coin to Mira.

Mira and Theos both held up their coins.

"It's the church!" Mira shouted. "The cross on the steeple matches the cross on the coin."

Theos extended his hand and lined up the coin with the outline of Mt. Zeus. "The cross lines up with Pastor Thomas's church," he agreed. "The star below the cross marks the shoreline just below the church."

"The jar!" Mira shouted. "That's where we found the jar."

"Andros said the star will lead you to the treasure," Theos said. "But the star doesn't lead to the treasure; it leads to the clues in the jar."

"So if the star doesn't mark the treasure . . ." Mira wondered aloud and then shouted, "The cross marks the spot! The cross must lead to the treasure!"

"Shh. Quiet!" Theos urged Mira. He looked around at the other passengers. They were all taking pictures of the coast. No one was aware the three had just discovered the location of the Captain's treasure.

"But where at the church?' Mira asked.

"Once we finish the clues, they will tell us," said Theos.

He couldn't wait to get back home and finish the clues.

"No need to worry," Mira said.

"What do you mean?" Theos asked.

"If someone searches for the treasure at the star, they will only find a broken jar. They will think someone beat them to the punch. We got there first," she said with a smile.

Theos smiled back and shouted, "Woo-hoo!" as he high-fived Mira.

The *Nerina* circled and headed back for the dock. Lydia took one last look at Mt. Zeus and fixed her eyes on the church below. She needed to speak with Pastor Thomas. He seemed to be connected to everything.

ACTS 15:36 — 21:16

• PART FOUR •

The Growth
of the Church

This section of Acts contains Paul's second and third missionary journeys. The opening comment by Paul to Barnabas reveals his purpose for another missionary trip: "Let us return and visit the brothers in every city where we proclaimed the word of the Lord, and see how they are" (Acts 15:36). Paul loved the people and the churches he planted. While on this return trip, the Spirit of God sent Paul to Macedonia to the city of Philippi where Paul preached the gospel. From there, Paul visited Thessalonica, Berea, Athens, and Corinth.

Paul's third missionary journey takes him to Ephesus. He returned to Macedonia, Greece and Troas. From there he traveled to Jerusalem. Paul was warned several times that danger awaited him in Jerusalem, and his friends urged him not to go. But Paul was determined to go and replied, "What are you doing, weeping and breaking my heart? For I am ready not only to be imprisoned but even to die in Jerusalem for the name of the Lord Jesus" (Acts 21:13). This section of Acts ends with Paul's arrival at Jerusalem.

Conflict

The fury of a tornado can split a tree in two. Though a great oak might stand strong for 100 years, the fierce wind of a twister can tear an oak apart. Christian friendships, like trees, can stand strong for years. But when a serious conflict blows in like a fierce storm, it can test the strength of any friendship. Life's trials can split the most mature Christian friends. That seems to be what happened to Barnabas and Paul.

In today's story, Paul and Barnabas fell into a disagreement they could not resolve. As they planned their journey, Barnabas wanted John Mark to join them. Paul, disappointed in Mark for not finishing their last mission, did not think it was a good idea. When Paul and Barnabas could not resolve their conflict, they went their separate ways.

The truth is we all struggle. We won't be made perfect until we get to heaven. This story helps us see that even mature Christians need the grace of God. If the Bible only spoke of perfect people who never made mistakes, we would all feel like we do not measure up. But seeing weakness in Paul and Barnabas can encourage us. Paul knew he was not perfect. He told Timothy he was the worst sinner of all (1 Timothy 1:15 NIV). He said that God displayed his perfect patience and mercy by saving him as an example for all who believe.

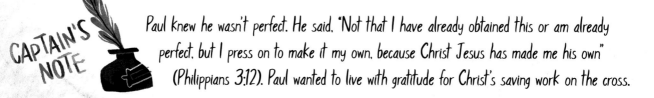

CAPTAIN'S NOTE

Paul knew he wasn't perfect. He said, "Not that I have already obtained this or am already perfect, but I press on to make it my own, because Christ Jesus has made me his own" (Philippians 3:12). Paul wanted to live with gratitude for Christ's saving work on the cross.

Watching over Us

It is fun to watch a parent teach their child to hit a baseball. They stand behind their child and hold the bat, waiting for the pitch. Then as the ball nears, they gently guide their child's swing to hit the ball. As soon as the ball flies off the bat, the parent shouts, "Run, you got a hit!" Their child runs with joy to first base, and once they safely arrive, they look back with delight. They hit the ball, but it was the parent's guiding hand that helped. Life as a Christian is like that. God our Father is ever watching over us, helping.

The apostle Paul was never alone on his missionary journeys. God was always with him. Here are a few examples: The Holy Spirit directed Paul away from Asia and Bithynia. Then the Lord gave Paul a vision of a man from Macedonia asking for help. Paul knew the vision was from God and immediately changed his plans to follow God's lead. Paul met a group of women in Macedonia and taught them. While Paul spoke, God worked in Lydia's heart (Acts 16:14). Paul was the one who shared the gospel, but it was God who opened Lydia's heart to believe.

The Holy Spirit still guides and helps us today. Jesus said, "When the Spirit of truth comes, he will guide you into all the truth" (John 16:13a). Paul taught, "let the Holy Spirit guide your lives. Then you won't be doing what your sinful nature craves" (Galatians 5:16 NLT). It is as though we are that child at the plate, and God has his hands on the bat to help us. While all our good works are only by his grace, God cheers us on.

READ Acts 16:16–40

God's Plan
Is Bigger

Sometimes bad things lead to good things. A work crew must cut down healthy trees to make room to build a road. The new road allows electric workers to add poles to carry power lines to rural communities, which improves travel. The cutting down of the trees might initially seem like a bad idea, but it often leads to good. The fallen trees can even be sent to the sawmill to make lumber to build new homes.

Even though bad things happened to Paul, God turned them into good. That is what happened in today's story. Paul was beaten and thrown into prison—that is the bad. But God had a plan to save the Philippian jailer and all of his household—that is how God worked it for good. Paul later taught the Romans, "we know that God causes everything to work together for the good of those who love God and are called according to his purpose" (Romans 8:28 NLT).

After his arrest and beating, Paul must have wondered, How can God work this together for good? But he received his answer after the earthquake, when the scared jailer asked, "What must I do to be saved?" Later, after another stay in prison, he told the Philippians, "I want you to know, brothers, that what has happened to me has really served to advance the gospel, so that it has become known throughout the whole imperial guard and to all the rest that my imprisonment is for Christ" (Philippians 1:12–13). So, when bad things happen to us, we can pray, "God, work them together for good." As we look back, we often see how God used the trials of our lives for our good and his glory.

Take a Close Look

If you look carefully at the wings of a butterfly, you will catch things others might miss. Its colorful wings are painted by thousands of multi-colored scales that shimmer in the light. The feather-like hairs and thousands of tiny facets on its compound eye, are astonishing! You won't notice these details unless you study the butterfly up close.

We have two groups of people in today's story: the Jews of Thessalonica and Berea. Those in Thessalonica rejected the message of the gospel. But the Jews in Berea were different. When Paul proclaimed the gospel to them, they opened their Bibles to take a closer look at the Scriptures. They examined the Bible closely, just as one studies a butterfly's wings. Luke writes that the Bereans "received the word with all eagerness, examining the Scriptures daily to see if these things were so. Many of them therefore believed" (Acts 17:11–12a).

If you study the Bible carefully, you will see all kinds of things that others miss. For example, long before Jesus was born, the prophet Isaiah foretold that Jesus would be born of a virgin and would be called Immanuel, which means "God with us" (Isaiah 7:14). It happened just as Isaiah said. The prophet Micah said Jesus would be born in Bethlehem (Micah 5:2), and he was. But most amazing is how the prophet Isaiah foretold of the crucifixion in Isaiah 53. Open your Bible to see for yourself. That is what the Bereans did. They studied the Bible and believed.

False Gods

CAPTAIN'S NOTE

God says idols are "gods of wood and stone, the work of human hands, that neither see, nor hear, nor eat, nor smell" (Deuteronomy 4:28). But our God is the living God (Jeremiah 10:10) who hears our prayers (1 Peter 3:12) and speaks to us through his Word (Hebrews 1:2).

It's fun to shape clay into objects and pretend they are alive. You can create figures with arms that move and heads that turn. Did you know that clay comes from large deposits in the ground? Did you know the very first man, Adam, was made from the dust of the ground? Genesis 2 gives us the details. It says, "the LORD God formed the man of dust from the ground and breathed into his nostrils the breath of life, and the man became a living creature" (v. 7). We can create figures from clay, but only God can make them come alive.

Paul told the people of Athens that the true God created all things, including people. And Paul said that God gave people life and breath. Paul observed that the city of Athens was full of idols. Idols are false gods that have no life. They are made of clay, wood, or metal. They can't move, for they have no breath of life in them. Idols can't help you. They are worthless, and yet many people around the world still worship idols because they don't know the true God and Creator.

Paul went on to urge the people to repent—to turn from worshiping worthless idols made by human hands. Paul told them about Jesus—the one who was raised from the dead and who would one day return to judge the earth. Some people mocked this idea, but several believed. What about you? Will you trust in the God who created people and gave them the breath of life, or will you trust in idols?

READ Acts 18:1–23

Corinth

In the spring, male bluebirds look for a good nesting site. When they find one, they stand upon it and call out to their mate, trying to persuade her to build a nest. The female bluebird will take a look. If the outside of the new home looks good, she will go inside to check it out. But if she doesn't like what she sees, she will reject it. In that case, the male bluebird must find another nesting site.

When Paul arrived at the city of Corinth, he went to the Jewish synagogue to tell the people that Jesus is the Christ, the Messiah the prophets promised God would send (Acts 18:5). Week after week, he tried to persuade them to believe, but they rejected his message. But Paul didn't give up. Just like the male bluebird looks for another home if the first is rejected, Paul left the Jewish synagogue and went to the home of a Gentile named Titus.

We know what Paul taught the Corinthians because he mentioned it in a letter. He wrote, "For what I received I passed on to you as of first importance: that Christ died for our sins according to the Scriptures, that he was buried, that he was raised on the third day according to the Scriptures" (1 Corinthians 15:3–4 NIV). Many of the Corinthians believed this gospel message and were baptized. Today, God calls us to believe that same message. As we do, we are called to share it with others, just like Paul did.

Ephesus

A signpost with the name of a town and an arrow tells you which way to go to reach that town. The signpost itself is not the town; it only points the way. Likewise, John the Baptist was not the promised Messiah. He was a signpost who pointed to Jesus. When people thought John might be the Promised One, he told them he was not (John 1:21). John said, "I baptize you with water for repentance. But after me comes one who is more powerful than I, whose sandals I am not worthy to carry. He will baptize you with the Holy Spirit" (Matthew 3:11 NIV). When Jesus came to be baptized, John told those gathered, "Behold, the Lamb of God, who takes away the sin of the world!" (John 1:29b). John pointed to Jesus.

The people at Ephesus knew about John's ministry, but no one had ever told them about Jesus. They didn't know that Jesus died for their sins or rose again. They didn't know about the Holy Spirit. When Paul realized this, he shared the gospel with them and they believed and were baptized. Then, as Paul prayed for them, something amazing happened. The Holy Spirit came upon them, just as John the Baptist foretold, and they began to speak in tongues (Acts 19:6).

After that, Paul remained in Ephesus for two years (Acts 19:10) and continued to share about Jesus with great power. People were healed and delivered from evil spirits. The new believers turned from their sins and evil ways and the word of the Lord continued to "increase and prevail mightily" (see Acts 19:18, 20).

Riot

If you have ever witnessed a hornet's nest being disturbed, you know to back away from the nest. The wasps quickly gather into a fierce, angry mob—ready to attack anything in their path. They stir each other up in fury. It takes time for them to settle down and return to their nest.

When Paul said the idols of Ephesus were fake (Acts 19:26), he made the idol makers angry. Demetrius, a silversmith, gathered the idol makers together and stirred them up into an angry mob. Some in the crowd didn't even know why they were rioting (Acts 21:30), but like a frenzy of buzzing wasps, they went on the attack. Paul wanted to calm them, but the disciples restrained him. They knew a mob would attack Paul too. Finally, after several hours, an official took control of the crowd.

Sometimes when we tell people that Jesus is the only way to heaven (John 14:6), they get angry. They don't like to be told they are wrong, or that they are following false gods. In these cases, it is best to be patient. While we can't change a person's heart, we can pray for God's name to be made known to them (Matthew 6:9). We can also continue loving them with the love of Christ.

CAPTAIN'S NOTE

Jesus told his followers they would face opposition. He said, "Remember the word that I said to you: 'A servant is not greater than his master.' If they persecuted me, they will also persecute you" (John 15:20).

READ Acts 20:7–16

Eutychus

Did you know that some animals sleep upside down? The sloth has long claws that hook around a tree limb to prevent it from falling during naps. Sloths spend up to eighteen hours a day sleeping upside down, and they never fall.

In today's story, Eutychus was not so fortunate. He could have used the sloth's claws the night Paul preached a sermon. It must have been hot in that third-floor room. So Eutychus sat on the ledge of an open window. When Paul's sermon went long, Eutychus drifted into a deep sleep, lost his balance, and fell out the window! The people rushing to help him, noticed he was dead! But Paul took Eutychus in his arms and healed him.

The story of Eutychus is similar to other stories in the Bible. Elisha raised a woman's son in the Old Testament (2 Kings 4:32–37), and Jesus raised Jairus's daughter from the dead during his ministry (Matthew 9:18–26). God was kind to confirm the truth of the gospel with powerful signs. Paul later wrote, "For we know, brothers loved by God, that he has chosen you, because our gospel came to you not only in word, but also in power and in the Holy Spirit and with full conviction" (1 Thessalonians 1:4–5a). Eutychus learned two lessons that night. First, never listen to a long sermon on a warm night from an open window. Second, the gospel is real and powerful to save.

READ Acts 20:17–38

It's More Blessed to Give

Which is more fun: getting a present, or giving one? It is exciting to open a present and see what is inside. But it is even more fun to watch a person open a gift you gave. In our story, Paul ended his message to the elders, repeating what Jesus taught, "It is more blessed to give than to receive" (Acts 20:35b).

Some gifts are so valuable you cannot buy them with money. For example, God the Father gave his only Son, Jesus. Jesus gave his life to take away our sin. The apostle Paul gave up his position as a Pharisee for a dangerous life preaching the gospel to Gentiles. Paul didn't preach to earn money; he worked as a tentmaker (Acts 20:33–34).

Even though Paul knew he would face hardship and prison, he didn't shrink back from his mission to go to Jerusalem to preach the gospel (Acts 20:22–23). When Ephesian pastors came to visit him, they warned him not to go. But nothing could stop Paul. He knew the mission must continue. So, after he knelt down with the pastors and prayed, Paul boarded the ship, and they returned home. Like Jesus, Paul gave his life away so that people could be saved.

CAPTAIN'S NOTE

One of the best Bible verses to memorize is about God's greatest gift. "For God so loved the world, that he gave his only Son, that whoever believes in him should not perish but have eternal life" (John 3:16).

CAPTAIN'S CLUE

SEARCH FOR THE ANSWER IN

ACTS PART FOUR: THE GROWTH OF THE CHURCH

CLUE:

Paul's friends warned him to stay,
but he knew he had to go.
So they knelt down and prayed,
before journeying back ho — —.

ho — — is the last part of the riddle.

Now let's put it together with what you have so far.

discover my treasure written in stone
after the Rock of Ages calls me ho — —

The Final Clue

Theos retrieved the piece of paper from his pocket and reread it as they climbed the rolling hills leading to the church.

"Discover my treasure, written in stone, after the Rock of Ages calls me home," he read aloud. "What do you think it means?"

"'Rock of Ages' is an old hymn," Lydia replied. "I'm not sure what the riddle means. But I do know one thing: Pastor Thomas has a lot of explaining to do."

"I sure hope he's home," said Mira.

Salty heard voices as they drew near. He barked and rushed through the tall grass to greet them. As they crested the last hill, Pastor Thomas waved his pruning shears, motioning for them to come. He stood under a large olive tree, beside a pile of pruned branches.

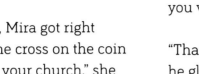

After a short greeting, Mira got right down to business. "The cross on the coin matches the cross on your church," she said, holding out the plastic doubloon. "We're here for the treasure."

"We've finished the book and have the final clue," Theos added as he handed the unfolded paper to the pastor.

Thomas took the paper. "So, you've gone through the journals and have come to the end," he said.

The children nodded in agreement.

"Which leads us to a question," said Lydia. "How did our names get into the journal? Andros said you had more to tell us."

"We also know you've read it before," Theos added. "You referenced the questions when you visited us."

"That's correct," Pastor Thomas replied as he glanced at the clue written on the page. "I've been looking forward to this day. Please have a seat." He motioned toward the benches. "Andros was right. There is much more to tell. Let's see. Where to start? Well, perhaps I will tell you about Theophilus."

Lydia and the children sat down and hung on every word.

"Captain Theophilus is your great uncle, Theos. He is your grandfather Philip's brother. He left the journals and scrolls to you just before he died. He passed away a month after your sister, Mira was born. That's when he added the note with your names. He asked me to tell you of the legend of the treasure and get you down to the ship, to lead you to the jar he concealed in the rocks. The one with the scrolls and journals inside. I was to start you on this quest to find the treasure when you turned twelve. But you two discovered the jar on your own."

"So, there is a treasure!" Theos could hardly contain his excitement.

"Peter never told me he had an uncle named Theophilus," Lydia remarked, surprised.

"Your grandfather Philip refused to mention his name and told the children Theophilus was a pirate who stole a ship from his father. Philip was like the older brother in the parable of the prodigal. He didn't like that your great-grandfather, Adamos, welcomed Theophilus back home. Then, when the rag caught fire and burned the pier, Philip blamed Theophilus."

Pastor Thomas continued, "Theophilus felt terrible. He insisted all the family money went to Philip, and kept only the *Providence*. Philip took the money, purchased your potato farm, and never spoke of his brother again.

"With the pier gone, Theophilus had nowhere to go. That was only a year and

a half after my wife, Gloria, passed on. So, I invited Theophilus to come and live with me here at the parsonage. Your uncle lived with me until the Lord called him home."

Theos snapped to attention. "That's it!" he shouted. "That's in the clue. Discover my treasure, written in stone, after the Rock of Ages calls me home." The last clue must be written on the Captain's gravestone."

"Not another clue," Pastor Thomas corrected Theos. "The gravestone is where you'll find the Captain's treasure. Let's go see." Theos sprang from the bench and ran to the cemetery beyond the tree. He scanned the headstones.

"Off to the right," Pastor Thomas instructed. Theos found the Captain's gravestone just as the others caught up.

Pastor Thomas read the stone aloud. It began with the Captain's last name, Adamos.

He then paused and continued reading the words of the hymn cut in stone:

Jesus, my highest treasure,
In Thy communion blest
I find unfailing pleasure,
True happiness and rest;
Myself a willing off'ring
I give to Thee alone,
Because by death and suff'ring
Thou didst for me atone

My Treasure is Christ

Captain Theophilus 1860—1940

"We should have guessed," Lydia said with tears running down her cheek. The Captain's treasure is Christ."

"Yes! He wanted to share it with you through his journals."

"What about the gold?" Theos asked. "What happened to all his gold?"

"You're standing on it!" Thomas answered.

"It's buried in the ground? Right here?" Theos exclaimed.

"No, Theos. It *is* the ground. The Captain used the gold to purchase all the land between the church and your farm, from the quarry in the hills, all the way to the sea. There are more than two thousand acres and he left it to you, your sister, and your mom. You're the richest family in all of Naxos. I've been waiting for the day I could tell you. The Captain's treasure is yours."

Theos looked down at the headstone, trying to make sense of it all. He reread the Captain's epitaph. He found the last words strangely comforting. He had been so eager to find the Captain's gold—he never considered finding another treasure.

Theos reread the words, "My treasure is Christ." Then he whispered, "My treasure is Christ." Then he shouted, "My treasure is Christ! My treasure is Christ!" He shouted so loudly that his words echoed off the cliffs!

In that moment, Theos believed the story of Jesus. For the first time, he realized that through the quest to find gold, he found an even greater treasure: Christ.

"Your uncle Theophilus is celebrating right now— Luke 15:7," said Pastor Thomas.

"Luke 15:7?" asked Lydia.

"Yes, 'there will be more joy in heaven over one sinner who repents than over ninety-nine righteous persons who need no repentance.' I'm certain your uncle is rejoicing right now!"

PART FIVE

Paul's Journey to Rome

In this last section of Acts, Paul is arrested and put on trial. As happened to Jesus, the officials do not believe that Paul is guilty, but the Jews are determined to kill him. They vow not to eat until Paul is dead. They plan to ambush Paul on his way to the Jewish court, but their plan is thwarted and Paul is sent to Governor Felix. Hoping for a bribe, Felix leaves Paul in prison, where he remains for several years.

When Festus takes over as governor, he plans to send Paul to Jerusalem to stand trial. Once again, the Jews plot to ambush Paul. But when Paul appeals for a trial in Rome, there is nothing to be done but send him to Rome. The book of Acts concludes with Paul's arrival in Rome. While the book ends suddenly, the mission of the gospel continued. You can discover more about what happened to Paul in the letters he later wrote. For example, in his letter to the Philippians, Paul mentions how God used his imprisonment to reach the Roman guards with the gospel (Philippians 1:12–13). So after you complete your voyage through Luke and Acts, you can continue your study by reading Paul's letters.

Danger Awaits in Jerusalem

When an enemy army attacks a city or a country, a call goes out for people to take up their swords and join the fight to defend their land. Those joining in battle know that they could lose their lives. Freedom comes at a cost. So why do they risk their lives? They know by fighting off the attack, they can save the lives of their families back home and preserve freedom for their land.

Paul knew he was engaged in a battle against the enemy. He told the Ephesians that we wage war against the powers of darkness and that the Word of God is our sword (Ephesians 6:10–17). The prophet Agabus warned Paul that he would be captured and turned over to the Gentiles (Acts 21:11). When Paul's friends heard this, they urged Paul not to go to Jerusalem (v. 12).

Paul replied, "I am ready not only to be imprisoned but even to die in Jerusalem for the name of the Lord Jesus" (Acts 21:13b). Paul told the Corinthians that he would rather die than silence the gospel (1 Corinthians 9:16–17). So, despite the danger, Paul continued on to Jerusalem, like a soldier going off to war. His mission was to bring freedom to the captives and salvation to all who would receive his message. A few days after he arrived in Jerusalem, he was arrested. But even in prison, Paul would not be silent.

Paul's Defense

A defense is something we use to protect ourselves from an attack. A soldier uses a shield as a defense against the enemy's sword. A stone wall of a castle is a defense against the enemy's advance.

When a person is arrested and stands before the court, they are given an opportunity to defend themselves against the charges. When Paul was arrested, he defended himself (Acts 22:1) by telling his story to the Roman tribune. Paul shared the story of how he met Jesus, hoping the tribune would believe him. But the Jews shouted against him and called for his death (v. 22). The tribune decided to whip Paul. He hoped this would reveal the real reason the Jews were upset.

But, before they could strike Paul with the whips, Paul had one last defense. He declared that he was a Roman citizen. He knew that Roman citizens could not be punished without a full trial (Acts 22:25). The centurion stopped in his tracks and reported this to the tribune. Once the tribune realized he had bound a Roman citizen, and ordered his flogging without a trial, he grew afraid. For now, Paul was safe, but he remained in captivity until the Romans made their next move.

CAPTAIN'S NOTE

The apostle Peter said we should always be ready to give a defense for why we believe in Jesus. He said, "Always [be] prepared to make a defense to anyone who asks you for a reason for the hope that is in you" (1 Peter 3:15).

The Plot to Kill Paul

A lone wolf could never take down a bull moose. As soon as the moose lowers its large rack of antlers, the wolf would run away. But a pack of wolves is different. While one wolf advances, another wolf in the pack attacks from behind. The Pharisees, Sadducees, chief priests and elders, along with a group of Jews, all ganged up on Paul like a pack of wolves. A group of more than forty Jewish men vowed they would not rest until they killed him.

Even though these men plotted to ambush Paul, God had greater plans. The Lord spoke to Paul and said, "Take courage, for as you have testified to the facts about me in Jerusalem, so you must testify also in Rome" (Acts 23:11). That meant the wolves would not succeed. God used a young man to defeat the Jews. Paul's nephew overheard their plan and sent word to the tribune. The tribune then sent 470 soldiers with Paul to the governor. The plot of the Jews against Paul was no match for our Almighty God.

We can trust God in our times of trouble too. Psalm 91 tells us, "Those who live in the shelter of the Most High will find rest in the shadow of the Almighty. This I declare about the LORD: He alone is my refuge, my place of safety; he is my God, and I trust him. For he will rescue you from every trap and protect you from deadly disease" (vv. 1–3 NLT).

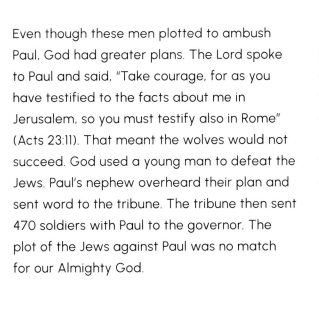

To Caesar

Have you ever heard someone say, "I have an ace to play"? Perhaps it is most commonly said while playing cards. After all, an ace is the most powerful card in the deck. But it can also be said if someone has a sure way out of a problem.

Guarded by more than 400 soldiers, Paul arrived safely in Caesarea to meet with Governor Felix. After questioning Paul, Felix held him captive for two years, hoping he would pay for his freedom (Acts 24:26). Felix allowed Paul's friends to come and go and care for Paul (v. 23). When Festus took over as governor, the Jews continued accusing Paul, wanting him dead. They asked Felix to grant them a favor—that Paul be sent to Jerusalem to stand trial. That would give them the chance to ambush Paul along the way.

When Felix questioned Paul, he suggested that Paul be sent to Jerusalem. When the Jews heard this, they assumed Felix had granted their favor. But Paul was not worried; he still had an ace to play. He was a Roman citizen. He could appeal to Caesar and request a trial in Rome. And that is just what he did. With his ace played, there was nothing the governor could do. Felix simply said, "To Caesar you have appealed; to Caesar you shall go" (Acts 25:12b). Paul's ace defeated the Jews and their evil plot. Paul was then sent to Rome, just as the Lord had said (Acts 23:11).

Paul Speaks to the King

Some events in our lives are so special that we want to tell everyone again and again. When a person sees a rainbow, they want to tell everyone about it. If you were to find a gold coin washed up on shore, you would show everyone. When a couple becomes engaged, they tell all their family and friends.

When Paul was given the opportunity to offer a defense before King Agrippa, he told the king the most important story of his life. Paul told him about the day he met Jesus. For Paul, that day was like seeing a rainbow, finding a treasure, and getting engaged, all wrapped up into one. For on that day, Paul met Jesus and discovered the treasure of forgiveness.

In writing the book of Acts, Luke didn't have to include Paul's whole story again. He could have simply said, "So Paul shared his testimony before King Agrippa." But Luke included the whole story again for a third time. He repeated it for us so that we get to hear the power of the gospel again and again and again. You see, Luke knew that Paul's treasure is our treasure too. For if we turn from our sin and place our trust in Jesus's death on the cross, we receive the same salvation and forgiveness as Paul. We join the bride of Christ, the family of God. And then best of all, one day in heaven we will see Jesus sitting upon his throne. "And he who sat there had the appearance of jasper and carnelian, and around the throne was a rainbow that had the appearance of an emerald" (Revelation 4:3).

READ Acts 27

The Shipwreck

A meteorologist is a person who studies the weather and makes predictions. They can tell us if it will be sunny or rainy outside. It is wise to listen to their advice, because they can see what will happen in the future. They study the air pressure, wind speed, and direction, and warn of concerns. If they urge you to take an umbrella to school, you should listen.

Paul had something better than a meteorologist to predict the weather in today's Bible story. Paul received his forecast from God. God revealed to Paul that terrible storms lay ahead. Paul then warned his guard and the crew, but they did not listen. They still set sail. Just as Paul predicted, a furious storm battered the ship for several days. The people aboard lost all hope of living (Acts 27:20). An angel of the Lord assured Paul that he would make it to Rome and everyone on board would survive. Paul told the others he had faith in God that it would be exactly as he had been told (v. 25). Just as Paul predicted, everyone made it safely to shore.

Did you know God has told us the future? And in doing so, he's also given us a warning. The Bible tells us that one day Jesus will return to judge everyone (2 Timothy 4:1). One day, each of us will stand before the judgment throne of God (Romans 14:10) to give an account of our lives. Those who rejected Jesus will be sent into the lake of fire (Revelation 20:15). But all those who turned from their sin to trust in Jesus will be welcomed into heaven to live with Jesus. He will wipe away our tears and make all things new (Revelation 21:3–5). Do you trust God's forecast? All who put their trust in Jesus will be kept safe, just like those aboard Paul's ship.

CAPTAIN'S NOTE

God has wonderful plans for each of his children. He even uses hardship for our good. He told Jeremiah, "For I know the plans I have for you, declares the Lord, plans for welfare and not for evil, to give you a future and a hope" (Jeremiah 29:11).

The End

A puzzle contains smaller pieces to a greater picture. To see the full picture, you need to assemble all the pieces together. A couple pieces might reveal a part of the puzzle, but they can't tell the whole story. The same is true of the Bible. The Bible is made up of sixty-six books written by more than thirty different authors living thousands of years apart. The books of Luke and Acts are like two puzzle pieces that tell the story of Jesus's ministry and the start of the church, but there is more to the story.

Luke ends the book of Acts with Paul imprisoned in Rome teaching about the Lord Jesus with "boldness and without hindrance" (Acts 28:31). But that is not the end of the story. If you want to find out more about what Paul preached and where he traveled, continue reading the New Testament. Many of the books after Acts are letters that he wrote to Christians living in various places in the ancient world.

When you are assembling a puzzle, looking at the photo on the box reveals what the end result will be. The book of Revelation is kind of like the picture on the puzzle box. It gives us the end picture. It says that Jesus is returning one day to judge the earth and make it new. The final words, "I am coming soon," are so important that Jesus repeats them three times (Revelation 22:7, 12, 20). Only those who treasure Christ and put their trust in Jesus, will be ready for his return and be welcomed into heaven. The books of Luke and Acts tell us all about Jesus and call us to believe, so we can be ready for his return.

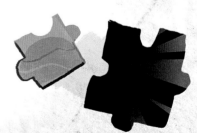

Jesus asked Martha a question we all need to answer. He said, "I am the resurrection and the life. Whoever believes in me, though he die, yet shall he live, and everyone who lives and believes in me shall never die. Do you believe this?" (John 11:25-26). Martha replied Yes. What about you?

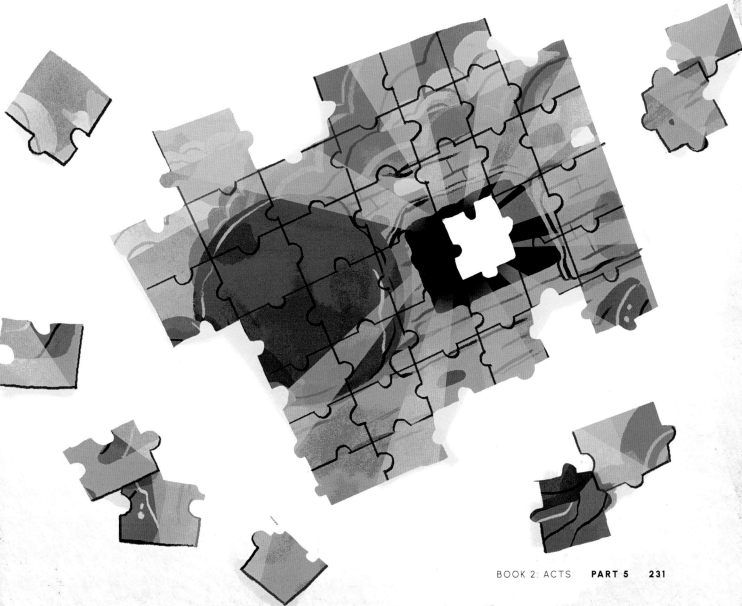

Lasting Treasure

Theos and Mira recounted their amazing journey in the weeks that followed the discovery of the treasure. It was hard to believe their quest was over. Andros was right, people with replica doubloons began hiking along the coast, in search of the treasure. The tours of the *Providence* sold out for weeks. Everyone wanted in on the treasure. Pastor Thomas posted a sign on the bluff, just above the location where he hid the water jar. It read: *"Discover my treasure, written in stone, after the Rock of Ages calls me home."* That led many explorers to the little church. Sunday attendance grew. While many of the first-time guests were tourists, a number of people joined the church and began attending weekly. Lydia, Theos, and Mira rarely missed a Sunday.

Pastor Thomas offered to lead Lydia and the kids through a weekly Bible study in their home. They gladly accepted. Over the months, Mira, Theos, and Lydia all made the treasure of Theophilus their own. Looking back, it was easy to see how God used their study of the scrolls and their search for the treasure to draw them into a relationship with Jesus. That was the Captain's plan all along. He knew a study of the gospel of Luke and the book of Acts had the power to change a person's life. After all, it changed his own.

Connecting Luke and Acts with the Old Testament

The day Jesus rose from the dead, he met two of his disciples on the road to Emmaus. Cleopas and his friend were confused and disappointed. They had heard Jesus's body was missing from the grave, but they did not recognize him walking with them on the road. Jesus chided them for not believing everything the prophets had spoken of. While they walked together, Jesus explained how the writings of Moses and the prophets pointed forward to him.

The two disciples were so excited to hear Jesus's words. Later, they said, "'Did not our hearts burn within us while he talked to us on the road, while he opened to us the Scriptures?'" (Luke 24:32).

Before returning to his Father in heaven, Jesus told the disciples to share his teaching everywhere (Matthew 28:20). The disciples obeyed his commission and told everyone they could how the Scriptures point to Jesus. Luke's gospel and the book of Acts preserve that teaching and give us a record of what Jesus taught on the road to Emmaus—how the Scriptures point to him.

In the following study, you will explore how Moses and the Old Testament prophets spoke of Jesus hundreds of years before his birth. As you read, pretend you are one of the disciples on your own journey to Emmaus. (Note: If possible, read the Scriptures from the ESV Bible. Read Scriptures marked NIV from the New International Version if you have one.)

Before you begin reading Scripture and answering questions, here are a few words you need to know:

PROPHECY – A message God gave a prophet to share with his people. Many prophecies point to something that will happen in the future.

FULFILLED – When something a prophet foretells comes true, we say the prophecy was fulfilled. That later event is called the fulfillment of the prophecy.

SHADOW – Some Old Testament events point forward to New Testament events. We say they are a "shadow" of things to come, which means they give us a hint of something God planned to do in the future. For example, the sacrifice of lambs for sin in the Old Testament is a shadow that points to Jesus's sacrifice on the cross. Every lamb slain is a shadow that points to the cross.

MESSIAH – This is the name given to the Son God promised to send to break the curse of sin and deliver God's people from their enemies. Messiah means anointed one. The Greek word for Messiah is Khristos, which is the same word we translate as Christ in English. So anytime Jesus is referred to as Christ, he is being called Messiah, the deliverer foretold by the prophets; the Son God promised would break the curse of sin.

Luke and the Old Testament

1. Read Luke 1:17a and Malachi 4:5–6.
How are the words the angel of the Lord spoke to Zechariah in Luke, like Malachi's prophecy?

2. Read Luke 1:26–27 and Isaiah 7:14.
How is the Luke passage a fulfillment of Isaiah's prophecy?

3. Read Luke 1:32–33 and 2 Samuel 7:12–13.
What are two ways that Gabriel's prophecy to Mary in Luke match Samuel's prophecy to King David?

4. Read Luke 2:4–5 and Micah 5:2.
How was Micah's prophecy fulfilled by Jesus's birth in Bethlehem?

5. Read Luke 3:2b–6 with Isaiah 40:3–5 and Malachi 3:1a.
John the Baptist taught the crowd that he was the one Isaiah said would come to prepare the way for Jesus. How does John also fulfill the prophecy in Malachi 3:1?

6. Read Luke 3:21–22 and Psalm 2:7.
How is Psalm 2:7 fulfilled by the words God the Father spoke over Jesus at his baptism?

7. Read Luke 3:33 and Genesis 49:10.
In his later years, Jacob gave a prophecy to his son Judah that is recorded in Genesis 49:10. How does Jesus fulfill this prophecy?

8. Read Luke 3:34 and Genesis 12:1–3.
Luke 3:34 is a portion of Jesus's family tree. In it, we see that Jesus came from the family line of Abraham, Isaac, Jacob, and Judah. God told Abram (Abraham) that all the families of the earth would be blessed through him. How is Jesus the fulfillment of that promise? Hint: Read Revelation 7:9.

9. Read Luke 4:16–21 and Isaiah 61:1–2a.
How do we know the passage from the scroll of Isaiah that Jesus read, was a prophecy about Jesus himself?

10. Read Luke 19:30, 35–38 and Zechariah 9:9.
Jesus instructs his disciples to bring him a donkey's colt, which he then rides into Jerusalem as he enters Zion (another name for Jerusalem). How is this a fulfillment of what Zechariah prophesied?

11. Read Luke 22:47–48 and Psalm 41:9.
How does David's prophecy point forward to Judas's betrayal of Jesus?

12. Read Luke 23:32–33 and Isaiah 53:12.
Luke tells us Jesus was crucified with two criminals. How is this a fulfillment of Isaiah's prophecy that foretold how the Messiah would be numbered with transgressors (sinners)?

13. Read Luke 23:34 with Psalm 22:16–18.
In Psalm 22, David clearly prophesied that people would cast lots for Jesus's clothing. What do you see in Psalm 22:16 that also speaks of Jesus's death on the cross?

14. Read Luke 23:35–37 and Psalm 22:6–8.
Psalm 22 is an amazing prophetic look ahead to the far-off day when Jesus would die on the cross. How is the mocking crowd at Jesus's crucifixion a fulfillment of David's prophecy in Psalm 22?

15. Read Luke 24:5b–7 and Psalm 16:10 NIV.
David prophesied that God would not abandon him to the "realm of the dead." Why do we know this cannot be about King David, but must be about someone else?

Acts and the Old Testament

16. Read Acts 1:9–11 and Psalm 24:7–10.
King David wrote Psalm 24. Bible scholars believe he wrote the psalm to celebrate moving the ark of the covenant to the city of Jerusalem. How does this psalm point forward to Jesus returning to heaven?

17. Read Acts 1:15–17, 20–22 NIV with Psalm 69:25; 109:8 NIV.
Without Peter making these connections, we might not have realized these verses point to Judas and the need of his replacement. (Maybe Jesus quoted these verses on the road to Emmaus, or taught them to the disciples before returning to heaven.) What happened to Judas that he needed to be replaced?

18. Read Acts 2:23–27 NIV and Psalm 16:9–11 NIV.
What clues do we have from Psalm 16 that point beyond King David to Jesus?

19. Read Acts 3:19–23 and Deuteronomy 18:15.
Moses said that one day God would send "a prophet like me." This was a hint that the promised Messiah would be a prophet. How does Jesus fulfill this word? How was Jesus a prophet?

20. Read Acts 4:11–12 and Psalm 118:22–23.
How was Jesus rejected by the people of Israel? (Hint: See Matthew 21:33–44.)

21. Read Acts 3:16; 4:24b–26 and Psalm 2:1–2.
When Peter and John healed the lame beggar at the temple, they were arrested. How is Acts 4 a fulfillment of Psalm 2:1–2?

22. Read Acts 8:32–34 and Isaiah 53:3–12.
Philip's conversation with the Ethiopian eunuch reveals something very important about Isaiah 53. It's all about Jesus! Which verses in Isaiah 53:3–12 point to Jesus's death on the cross?

23. Read Acts 13:22–23 and Isaiah 9:6–7.
What hints do we have in Isaiah's prophecy that the promised offspring of David was fulfilled by Jesus?

24. Read Acts 13:14b–15, 32–33 and Psalm 2:7–8.
How do we know Psalm 2 is about Jesus?

25. Read Acts 13:34 and Isaiah 55:3.
Isaiah 52—53 is a prophecy about Jesus's sacrificial death. How could Isaiah, who lived 700 years before Jesus was born, write such a clear prophecy describing Jesus?

26. Acts 13:35–37 NIV and Psalm 16:9–10 NIV. Peter used this same Old Testament connection in Acts 2 when he taught those gathered for the feast of Pentecost. Here Paul also connects Psalm 16 to Jesus. What hints do we have that David placed his hope in God's future plan?

27. Read Acts 13:38–41 and Habakkuk 1:5. The prophet Habakkuk warned that not everyone would believe in Jesus. How does that warning apply to us today?

28. Read Acts 13:47–48 with Isaiah 49:6; also read Acts 15:16–18 with Amos 9:11–12. After hearing that God was touching Gentiles and filling them with the Holy Spirit, James quoted the prophet Amos. Amos foretold of a day when God would reach the nations beyond Israel. How is this good news for us today?

29. Read Acts 28:26–28 and Isaiah 6:9–10. Paul taught from morning until evening, trying to convince the Jews that Jesus was the Messiah from the Old Testament. He shared the same connections Jesus taught his followers on the road to Emmaus. Why is Paul's warning to the unbelieving Jews important for us today?

Answer Key

Luke and the Old Testament

1. Read Luke 1:17a and Malachi 4:5–6.
ANSWER 1. Malachi said that God would send Elijah to turn the hearts of the fathers to their children. The angel of the Lord tells us that Zechariah's son, John the Baptist, is the one God promised to send.

2. Read Luke 1:26–27 and Isaiah 7:14.
ANSWER 2. Isaiah foretold that God's promised Messiah would be born to an unmarried woman [a virgin]. Mary was a virgin, for she was not yet married to Joseph when Jesus was born. Isaiah also said that the one to come would be called Immanuel, which means God with us. The angel told Mary her son would be called Son of the Most High [Son of God]. That means God's Son would come to earth to be with us—God with us, Immanuel (see also Matthew 1:23).

3. Read Luke 1:32–33 and 2 Samuel 7:12–13.
ANSWER 3. The promised Son would be a son of King David and would sit on his throne forever to reign over an everlasting Kingdom. Even though King David's son Solomon ruled on his throne, and so did his sons after him, only Jesus reigns forever. So, this prophecy points to him.

4. Read Luke 2:4–5 and Micah 5:2.
ANSWER 4. Micah foretold that a ruler of Israel would come from Bethlehem, and Jesus is that ruler. Micah said the ruler would be one who was foretold "from of old, from ancient days." That is a reference to God's Messiah, not just any ruler.

5. Read Luke 3:2b–6 with Isaiah 40:3–5 and Malachi 3:1a.
ANSWER 5. John is the messenger that God sent to prepare the people to receive Jesus. (Also read Luke 3:10–22 to see how John prepared the way for the ministry of Jesus))

6. Read Luke 3:21–22 and Psalm 2:7.
ANSWER 6: Psalm 2 describes the Messiah (called the Lord's "anointed" in verse two). Verse seven tells us that he would also be God's Son. When God the Father called Jesus his "beloved Son" at his baptism, it fulfilled the prophecy of Psalm 2.

7. Read Luke 3:33 and Genesis 49:10.
ANSWER 7. Judah was the far-off grandfather of Jesus. The scepter, which is a sign of kingship and rule, will be with Jesus for all eternity, just as Jacob had prophesied.

8. Read Luke 3:34 and Genesis 12:1–3.
ANSWER 8. In Revelation 7:9, we read that people who believe in Jesus will be gathered from all nations before the throne. In this we see that all the nations are blessed through Jesus.

9. Read Luke 4:16–21 and Isaiah 61:1–2a.
ANSWER 9. Jesus did what the prophecy foretold. He healed the sick, set the demon possessed free, and preached the good news of the gospel to thousands. What's more, after he finished reading, Jesus told the people, "Today this Scripture has been fulfilled in your hearing" (Luke 4:21).

10. Read Luke 19:30, 35–38 and Zechariah 9:9.
ANSWER 10. Zechariah called the people of Zion to shout when their king came into the city on a colt. When Jesus came into the city riding the colt, the people shouted, calling him "King." That matches what Zechariah said would happen.

11. Read Luke 22:47–48 and Psalm 41:9.
ANSWER 11. Judas was welcomed into Jesus's

close circle of friends, the disciples. Betraying Jesus with a kiss shows how close he was to the Lord and yet, Judas did not really love Jesus.

12. Read Luke 23:32–33 and Isaiah 53:12.
Answer 12. "Numbered with transgressors" is another way of saying "in the same group with sinners." Three men were crucified that day: Jesus and two criminals. If anyone were to ask how many were crucified, the response would be, "They crucified three, Jesus and two criminals." So, Jesus was numbered with the transgressors.

13. Read Luke 23:34 with Psalm 22:16–18.
ANSWER 13. The Roman soldiers nailed Jesus's hands and feet to the cross. (See also John 20:25.) This matches David's description in Psalm 22:16.

14. Read Luke 23:35–37 and Psalm 22:6–8.
ANSWER 14. David said people would mock or scoff at God's chosen one, and that is exactly what they did to Jesus on the cross.

15. Read Luke 24:5b–7 and Psalm 16:10 NIV.
ANSWER 15. King David died and was buried. His body decayed, returning to the dust of the earth. Jesus died and was buried, but he rose from the dead. His body never saw decay.

Acts and the Old Testament

16. Read Acts 1:9–11 and Psalm 24:7–10.
ANSWER 16. After his death, Jesus was lifted up to heaven. David was king over Israel; Jesus is King over all heaven and earth. So, while this might have been written to celebrate David's victory in returning the ark to Jerusalem, it also points to Jesus who reigns over all.

17. Read Acts 1:15–17, 20–22 NIV with Psalm 69:25; 109:8 NIV.
ANSWER 17. Judas betrayed Jesus and afterward took his own life.

18. Read Acts 2:23–27 NIV and Psalm 16:9–11 NIV.
ANSWER 18. David died and was buried, and his body returned to dust. But the psalm says, "'You will not let your holy one see decay.'" That could not be talking about King David's body. Also, the name, Holy One, was another way of saying God's Messiah (see Mark 1:24).

19. Read Acts 3:19–23 and Deuteronomy 18:15.
ANSWER 19. A prophet is someone who speaks God's words to the people. While Jesus was fully man, he was more than a man—he was also fully God. Jesus didn't just bring a

prophetic word from God; Jesus is called the Word of God. In the first chapter of his gospel, John calls Jesus the Word of God that came to us. After Jesus raised the widow's son in Luke 7:16, the people called him a great "prophet."

20. Read Acts 4:11–12 and Psalm 118:22–23.
ANSWER 20. The religious rulers were jealous of Jesus and crucified him. In Matthew 21:33–44, Jesus told the religious rulers the parable of the vineyard in which the people who rent the vineyard kill the owner's son. In connecting this parable to Psalm 118:22, Jesus was saying that he himself was the son in the parable, and the religious rulers who were listening were the tenants who killed him. As Jesus spoke, the chief priests and Pharisees realized Jesus was talking about them. And just like the tenants plotted to kill the son in the parable, the religious rulers plotted to kill Jesus, the Son of God.

21. Read Acts 3:16; 4:24b–26 and Psalm 2:1–2.
ANSWER 21. Peter and John said that it was not by their power that the lame man was healed. They spoke about Jesus, saying, "The faith that is through Jesus has given the man this perfect health . . ." [Acts 3:16]. The religious rulers arrested Peter and John because they were against Jesus and anyone teaching about him. So, they set themselves against Jesus, the Anointed One, just as Psalm 2 predicted.

22. Read Acts 8:32–34 and Isaiah 53:3–12.
ANSWER 22. Isaiah 53 points to Jesus's death on the cross: Jesus was rejected by men (verse 3); on the cross, Jesus's hands and feet were pierced by nails (verse 5); Jesus took our sin (verses 5 and 6); Jesus was buried in a rich man's tomb (verse 9); Jesus was killed as an offering for our sin (verse 10); we are made righteous by the death of Jesus (verse 11); Jesus was crucified between two criminals (transgressors) (verse 12); and Jesus died for the sins of everyone who trusts in him (verse 12).

23. Read Acts 13:22–23 and Isaiah 9:6–7.
ANSWER 23. Isaiah says "a son" will be given who will be called "Mighty God." Isaiah also says this king's throne will go on forever. Every king in the line of David died and gave up his throne to another. Only Jesus sits on an everlasting throne. His kingdom and rule will never end.

24. Read Acts 13:14b–15, 32–33 and Psalm 2:7–8.
ANSWER 24. When Paul preached in the synagogue in Antioch (Acts 13:14–15), he explained that Psalm 2 pointed to Jesus. Anytime the Bible connects something from the New Testament with a prophecy in the Old Testament, we know that it is true.

25. Read Acts 13:34 and Isaiah 55:3.
ANSWER 25. The Spirit of God told the prophets what would take place and inspired them to write it down for us. First Peter 1:12 says, "It was revealed to them that they were serving not themselves but you, in the things that have now been announced to you through those who preached the good news to you by the Holy Spirit sent from heaven, things into which angels long to look."

26. Read Acts 13:35–37 NIV and Psalm 16:9–10 NIV.
ANSWER 26. David placed his hope in God's future plan when he wrote, "My heart is glad and my tongue rejoices" (Psalm 16:9a).

27. Read Acts 13:38–41 and Habakkuk 1:5.
ANSWER 27. Just as in Paul's day, people refuse to believe and trust in Jesus for the forgiveness of their sin. Each of us must decide: Are we going to believe and trust in Jesus, or will we reject him?

28. Read Acts 13:47–48 with Isaiah 49:6; also read Acts 15:16–18 with Amos 9:11–12.
ANSWER 28. Most Christians today are not Jewish, which means we are Gentiles or non-Jews. If God had not opened a way to save people from every nation, only Jewish believers would go to heaven. But Jesus came so that whoever believes in him would not perish but have everlasting life (John 3:16).

29. Read Acts 28:26–28 and Isaiah 6:9–10.
ANSWER 29. When we see the Old Testament connections that foretold of Jesus, we have the same choice to make. Will we believe and put our trust in Jesus, or will we reject him? The Bible points to Jesus and his death on the cross as the only way to be saved. The question is: Will we turn from our sin and believe in Jesus, or will we reject him?

ENDNOTES

76   Gold facts from https://www.visualcapitalist.com/12-stunning-visualizations-of-gold-bars-show-its-rarity, accessed March 5, 2023.
103   Points in "Luke, Part Five" are drawn from Darrell L. Bock, *Luke Volume 2: 9:51–24:53* (Grand Rapids, MI: Baker Academic, 1996), 1569.
106   Josephus quoted in William Whiston and Paul L. Maier, *The New Complete Works of Josephus.* (Grand Rapids, MI: Kregel, 1999), 109.
145   Bay of Fundy facts from https://www.bayoffundy.com/about/highest-tides, accessed March 5, 2023.
217   "Jesus My Highest Treasure," Salomon Liscovius, 1672. Translator, Frederick William Foster, 1789.

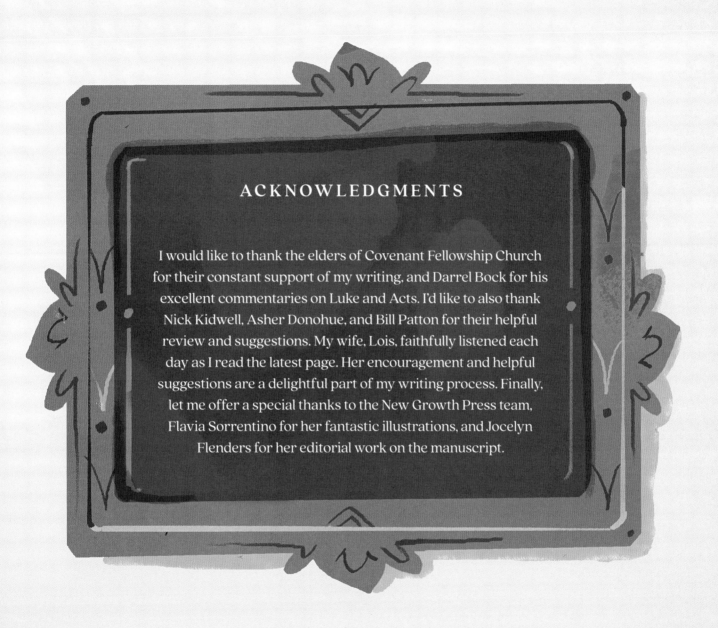

ACKNOWLEDGMENTS

I would like to thank the elders of Covenant Fellowship Church for their constant support of my writing, and Darrel Bock for his excellent commentaries on Luke and Acts. I'd like to also thank Nick Kidwell, Asher Donohue, and Bill Patton for their helpful review and suggestions. My wife, Lois, faithfully listened each day as I read the latest page. Her encouragement and helpful suggestions are a delightful part of my writing process. Finally, let me offer a special thanks to the New Growth Press team, Flavia Sorrentino for her fantastic illustrations, and Jocelyn Flenders for her editorial work on the manuscript.

More great resources by Marty Machowski

The Ology is a stunningly illustrated beginner's theology book to help kids of
all ages understand who God is and how we, as his children, relate to him.

————

Your children may know of the psalms, but with *WonderFull* young
readers learn to use the whole book of the Psalms to pray, worship,
and find help through the challenges life is certain to bring.